Ethiopia:

Malaria Operational Plan FY 2014

Table of Contents

ACRONYMS & ABBREVIATIONS

ACT	Artemisinin-based combination therapy
AL	Artemether-lumefantrine
ANC	Antenatal care
APS	Annual Program Statements
CBO	Community-based organization
CDC	Centers for Disease Control and Prevention
CJTF-HOA	US Department of Defense "Combined Joint Task Force-Horn of Africa"
CNHDE	Center for National Health Development in Ethiopia
DDT	Dichloro-diphenyl-trichloroethane
DHS	Demographic and Health Survey
EHNRI	Ethiopian Health and Nutrition Research Institute
ESR	Epidemic Surveillance and Response
FANC	Focused antenatal care
FELTP	Field Epidemiology and Laboratory Training Program
FMHACA	Food, Medicine and Health Care Administration and Control Authority
FMOH	Federal Ministry of Health
GHI	Global Health Initiative
Global Fund	Global Fund to Fight AIDS, Tuberculosis and Malaria
GoE	Government of Ethiopia
HDA	Health development army
HEP	Health extension package
HEW	Health extension worker
HMIS	Health management information system
HSDP	Health Sector Development Plan
iCCM	Integrated community case management
IPTp	Intermittent preventive treatment of pregnant women
IRS	Indoor residual spraying
ITN	Insecticide-treated bed net
LLIN	Long-lasting insecticidal net
MCST	Malaria Control Support Team
M&E	Monitoring and Evaluation
MIS	Malaria Indicator Survey
MNCH	Maternal and Neonatal Child Health
MOP	Malaria Operational Plan
NGO	Nongovernmental organization
NMCP	National Malaria Control Program
ORHB	Oromia Regional Health Bureau
PEPFAR	President's Emergency Plan for AIDS Relief
PFSA	Pharmaceutical Fund and Supply Agency
PHEM	Public Health Emergency Management
PLMP	Pharmaceutical Logistics Master Plan
PMI	President's Malaria Initiative

PMTCT	Prevention of mother-to-child transmission
QA/QC	Quality assurance/quality control
RBM	Roll Back Malaria
RDT	Rapid diagnostic test
RHB	Regional Health Bureau
SBCC	Social behavior change communication
SNNPR	Southern Nations, Nationalities and People's Regional State
TAC	Technical Advisory Committee
TFM	Transitional Funding Mechanism
UNICEF	United Nations Children's Emergency Fund
USAID	United States Agency for International Development
USG	United States Government
WHO	World Health Organization

EXECUTIVE SUMMARY

Malaria prevention and control are major foreign assistance objectives of the U.S. Government (USG). The purpose of this Malaria Operational Plan (MOP) is to provide a framework and a rationale for nominating and supporting malaria prevention and control projects in Ethiopia with FY 2014 funding to accomplish the USG's foreign assistance objectives through the President's Malaria Initiative (PMI) in the context of the Global Health Initiative (GHI). Through the GHI, the USG will help partner countries improve health outcomes, with a particular focus on improving the health of women, newborns, and children. The MOP process for PMI Year 7 (FY 2014) considers information from the Ethiopian Federal Ministry of Health (FMOH), Regional Health Bureaus including the Oromia Regional Health Bureau (ORHB), international malaria program donors including the Global Fund to Fight AIDS, Tuberculosis and Malaria (Global Fund), malaria subject matter experts, and other malaria program stakeholders about the malaria situation, and the malaria control program capacities and gaps in Ethiopia.

The President's Malaria Initiative is a core component of the GHI, along with health programs for HIV/AIDS and Tuberculosis; PMI was launched in June 2005 to rapidly scale up malaria prevention and treatment interventions and reduce malaria-related mortality by 50% in selected high-burden countries in sub-Saharan Africa. Other PMI goals include removing malaria as a major public health problem, promoting development in the Africa region, strengthening malaria control activities, and containing the spread of antimalarial drug resistance. The programming of PMI activities follows the core principles of GHI: encouraging country ownership and investing in country-led plans and health systems; increasing impact and efficiency through strategic coordination and programmatic integration; strengthening and leveraging key partnerships, multilateral organizations, and private contributions; implementing a woman- and girl-centered approach; improving monitoring and evaluation; and promoting research and innovation.

Malaria is ranked as the leading communicable disease in Ethiopia, accounting for about 30% of the overall Disability Adjusted Life Years lost. Approximately 68% of the total population of 84.3 million lives in areas at significant risk of malaria. According to the FMOH, in 2010/2011, malaria was the leading cause of outpatient visits, accounting for 15% of all visits, and health facility admissions, with 15% of all admissions. Malaria is one of the top ten causes of in-patient deaths among children less than five years of age and adults.

President's Malaria Initiative support to malaria prevention and control in Ethiopia began in FY 2008 with an initial focus on Oromia Regional State, the largest of Ethiopia's nine regional states, covering a third of the country. Ethiopia has received four malaria grants from the Global Fund in recent years. PMI has contributed between $20 and $43 million annually to malaria control efforts in Ethiopia during the last five years. With this support and that of other donors, the Government of Ethiopia (GoE)'s FMOH has been able to dramatically scale-up its efforts in malaria prevention and control in the last decade.

The most recent Malaria Indicator Survey (MIS), in 2011, showed that the prevalence of malaria parasitemia was approximately one percent, and that long-lasting insecticide treated net (LLIN) ownership had dramatically increased from the baseline in 2000, but was still below target levels. Historically, Ethiopia has experienced cycles of malaria epidemics every five to eight years, with the last nationwide epidemic in 2003.

The activities PMI proposed with FY 2014 funding will complement the FMOH's National Strategic Plan for Malaria Prevention and Control 2011-2015, and build on investments made by the GoE and other partners over the past ten years. While the primary focus continues to be on Oromia Regional State, PMI gradually expanded support nationwide since FY 2011 and will continue to expand these activities with FY 2014 funding. The proposed FY 2014 PMI budget for Ethiopia is $37 million. Outlined below are the FY 2014 budget's major components, which envisage sustaining and expanding PMI support to most ongoing activities.

Insecticide-treated nets (ITNs): Between 2005 and 2012, about 51 million ITNs were distributed in mass campaigns by the FMOH nationwide, including 5.9 million LLINs purchased by PMI, with most of the other LLINs purchased through Global Fund grants. With FY 2014 funding, PMI will procure 2.1 million additional LLINs that will be distributed mainly by mass campaigns through community based distribution channels. The LLIN distribution will be complemented by comprehensive social behavior change communication efforts to ensure that ITN use by the population is maximized. PMI will also provide support for national net coverage efforts by supporting national malaria commodity microplanning activities, which estimate district and community-level ITN needs and gaps.

Indoor Residual Spraying (IRS): With earlier funding, PMI supported Ethiopia's long-standing and extensive IRS program through a comprehensive range of activities, including improved targeting and enumeration of areas for IRS operations, improved IRS commodity and insecticide procurement, distribution and storage systems, training and supervision of spray personnel and appropriate pesticide management, entomological monitoring, and environmental compliance. With FY 2014 funding PMI will provide comprehensive IRS support by spraying approximately 550,000 structures in 36 districts protecting an estimated 1.5 million residents and will provide partial support to 24 graduated districts that previously had been fully supported by PMI. PMI also will continue to support building the capacity of the regional, zonal, and district-level vector control specialists to conduct basic entomological monitoring and improve IRS targeting and implementation as well as improve pesticide management.

Malaria in Pregnancy: Because of the generally low transmission of malaria in Ethiopia, intermittent preventive treatment of pregnant women is not a part of the national strategy. Universal ITN coverage is promoted, giving special emphasis and priority to ITN use among pregnant women, and prompt diagnosis and treatment of clinical cases when they occur. With FY 2014 funding, PMI will support improved malaria case management for pregnant women through an integrated approach to fever management at the community level provided by health extension workers (HEWs) and expanded access to high-quality antenatal care through health centers. Also, PMI will promote expanded and improved malaria in pregnancy case management services through safe motherhood and focused antenatal care pre- and in-service trainings for HEWs and midwives.

Case Management: PMI assisted the FMOH in updating the national malaria case management guidelines in 2012. These guidelines reinforced the importance of confirmatory diagnostic testing for all suspected malaria cases, with microscopy at health facility level and RDTs at community level. The most recently available microplanning data revealed that over 80% of clinically suspected malaria cases had a laboratory test confirmed diagnosis with microscopy or RDTs, and the number of empirically treated patients has declined, with the avoidance of artemisinin-based combination therapy (ACT) wastage. The guidelines also revised recommendations for severe disease management, promoting rectal artesunate for pre-referral treatment and intravenous artesunate for inpatient management. PMI has expanded support for quality-assured diagnostic testing for malaria to over 500 clinical laboratories in Oromia and regional labs in Amhara, Dire Dawa, SNNPR, and Tigray. PMI supports training and clinical supervision strengthening activities for HEWs in over 301 districts in six Regional States. PMI also supports provision of supplies, training, supervision, and implementation of quality assurance/quality control systems to improve the quality and accuracy of malaria diagnosis and clinical management of fever, while providing sufficient quantities of RDTs and ACTs to meet all requirements for Oromia and fill gaps in other regional states. PMI also procures enough chloroquine, rectal artesunate, and intravenous artesunate to meet national requirements.

President's Malaria Initiative also is strengthening the pharmaceutical management system, including procurement, warehousing, and delivery of malaria commodities, in line with the national Pharmaceutical Logistics Master Plan (PLMP) through the Pharmaceutical Funding and Supply Agency. PMI also is supporting the ORHB and its expanding system of HEWs to promote early care-seeking behavior and adherence to malaria drug treatment. PMI support also has been provided to the Ethiopian Food, Medicine, and Health Care Administration and Control Authority to ensure that all malaria products entering the country meet quality standards. Four of the ten anti-malarial drug efficacy monitoring sites throughout the country are being supported by PMI in Oromia.

With FY 2014 funding, PMI will procure and distribute 6 million multi-species RDTs, 220 microscopes, 3.8 million ACT treatments, 1.5 million chloroquine treatments (for treatment of *Plasmodium vivax*), together with drugs for severe disease and pre-referral care. In addition, PMI's quality assurance activities will be expanded to additional laboratories in Oromia and to the remaining regional state reference laboratories.

Epidemic Surveillance / Monitoring and Evaluation: With malaria prevalence low and decreasing in some places, improved data and information management for operations in Ethiopia, tracking both the focal malaria burden and the local status of malaria related commodities and operations will be of great importance. To improve routine surveillance, PMI is assisting the FMOH in the enhancement of the newly updated Public Health Emergency Management system together with the Health Management Information System for routine collection of facility-based data, and is supporting a scalable epidemic detection system to capture indicators beyond routine surveillance data, and track morbidity and mortality to evaluate program progress and effectiveness.

With FY 2014 funding, this support will be sustained, together with efforts to monitor malaria morbidity, mortality, and availability of malaria commodities at the district level. This complements support for nationwide, district-level ('bottom-up') malaria commodities microplanning to ensure that commodity procurements and distributions match district-level needs and are reaching beneficiaries. With FY 2014 funding, PMI will continue to support three staff enrolled in the Field Epidemiology and Laboratory Training Program and will increase regular on-site support and technical assistance to the Ethiopian Health and Nutrition Research Institute.

Health Systems Strengthening and Integration: As one of the GHI Plus Countries, PMI in Ethiopia is fully aligned with the GHI principles of building country capacity and integrating across programs. PMI provides significant support to Ethiopia's Health Extension Program that includes 30,000 HEWs staffing 15,000 health posts that provide curative and preventive services for a range of health conditions including malaria, at the community level. With FY 2014 funding, PMI will continue its support for integrated training and supervision of HEWs and for development of their capacity to detect malaria outbreaks in their catchment population. In addition, PMI and PEPFAR will continue to provide the majority of the support for implementing the PLMP and strengthening Ethiopia's pharmaceutical management system. The PMI-supported initiative on microplanning for malaria commodities is building capacity for forecasting commodity requirements and monitoring consumption at national, regional, and district levels. These skills can easily be used to forecast and monitor other essential health commodities. In addition, PMI support has helped to improve the capacity within Ethiopia to conduct entomologic surveillance and monitor insecticide resistance. Lastly, PMI is leveraging support through PEPFAR to strengthen laboratory diagnosis of malaria, in conjunction with strengthening of laboratory capacity to diagnose tuberculosis and HIV infections.

Social and Behavioral Change Communication (SBCC) : The Ethiopian Health Extension Program (HEP) provides malaria prevention and control information and conducts SBCC activities in nearly all malaria-endemic communities. The Health Development Armies (HDAs) supports HEWs to increase contact with each household through networking one to five households to deliver malaria messages. During 2013, PMI supported training in SBCC of 11,760 HDA members and community leaders, 771 health providers, and 1,256 HEWs. During the first half of 2013, 1,781, 614 SBCC materials have been distributed, reaching 96,755 households. In addition, a total of 2,512 students have been reached through school clubs and another 26,180 students through school mini-media in a total of 60 schools. With FY 2014 funding, malaria SBCC activities will be more integrated and coordinated with other health behavioral change communication (BCC) activities such as the maternal, newborn, and Child Health (MNCH) and family planning and reproductive health programs. PMI will also support local organizations through an Annual Program Statement (APS) mechanism to build local capacity in malaria key message communications.

STRATEGY

INTRODUCTION

Malaria prevention and control are major foreign assistance objectives of the U.S. Government (USG). The purpose of this Malaria Operational Plan (MOP) is to provide a framework and a rationale for supporting malaria prevention and control projects in Ethiopia with FY 2014 funding to accomplish the USG's foreign assistance objectives. Previously published MOP documents available on www.pmi.gov were used as references to develop this document for Ethiopia. Proposed PMI Ethiopia FY 2014 funding is contingent on USG official approval processes; any approved PMI FY 2014 funding will likely be unavailable for authorized expenditures until late 2014. The MOP process considers information from the Ethiopian Federal Ministry of Health (FMOH), international malaria program donors including the Global Fund to Fight AIDS, Tuberculosis and Malaria (Global Fund), malaria subject matter experts, and other malaria program stakeholders about the malaria situation, and the malaria control program capacities and gaps in Ethiopia.

The President's Malaria Initiative (PMI) was launched in June 2005 as a 5-year, $1.2 billion inter-agency initiative to rapidly scale up malaria prevention and treatment interventions and to reduce malaria-related mortality by 50% in 15 high-burden countries in sub-Saharan Africa. The USG announced Ethiopia as a PMI focus country in 2007, supported by $20 million in PMI funding beginning in FY 2008. PMI support was initially targeted to malaria control activities in the Oromia Regional State, which has about one-third of Ethiopia's malaria burden, population, and land area. Together with both Global Fund and PMI funding and the support from other donors and partners, the Government of Ethiopia (GoE)'s FMOH has been able to dramatically scale-up its efforts in malaria prevention and control since 2005.

In May 2009, President Barack Obama announced the Global Health Initiative (GHI), a multi-year, comprehensive USG effort to reduce the burden of disease and promote healthy communities and families around the world. Through the GHI, the USG provides assistance to partner countries to improve health outcomes, with a particular focus on improving the health of women, newborns, and children. PMI immediately became a core component of the GHI, along with the USG's global health programs for HIV/AIDS (the President's Emergency Program for AIDS Relief, PEPFAR) and tuberculosis and including the USG's support for Global Fund. The USG closely aligned its support for PMI, PEPFAR, and Global Fund through various steering and oversight committees and with coordinated funding processes within the GHI framework.

With passage of the 2008 Lantos-Hyde Act, funding for PMI was extended and, as part of the GHI, the goal of PMI was adjusted to reduce malaria-related mortality by 70% in the original 15 countries by the end of 2015.

The programming of PMI activities has been aligned to follow the core principles of GHI: encouraging country ownership and investing in country-led plans and health systems; increasing impact and efficiency through strategic coordination and programmatic integration; strengthening and leveraging key partnerships, multilateral organizations, and private contributions; implementing a woman- and girl-centered approach; improving monitoring and evaluation; and promoting research and innovation. In June 2010, the USG selected Ethiopia as one of the first eight 'GHI Plus' countries, involving comprehensive, multi-sectorial approaches to USG global health development including PMI's support for malaria control and prevention. Since 2011, PMI annual budgets for Ethiopia increased to approximately $40 million annually to allow more support for malaria activities beyond the borders of Oromia Regional State.

Malaria is ranked as the leading communicable disease in Ethiopia, accounting for about 30% of the overall Disability Adjusted Life Years lost. Approximately 57.3 million (68%) of the 84.3 million population of Ethiopia live in areas at risk of malaria. According to the FMOH, malaria was the leading cause of outpatient visits and health facility admissions in 2010/2011, accounting for 15% of reported outpatient visits and nearly 15% of admissions. Malaria also was among the ten leading causes of inpatient deaths among children less than five years of age. Because of a weak (but rapidly improving) malaria disease surveillance system and the inability of the Health Management Information System (HMIS) to capture all necessary malaria related indicators, official estimates of the true burden of malaria in Ethiopia are imprecise, and the completed HMIS surveillance reports are often more than one year old when published.

Previous PMI MOPs for Ethiopia highlighted unique aspects of malaria in Ethiopia, including the PMI geographical focus; Ethiopia's long history of commitment to malaria control; the structure of the health care system; the community-level Health Extension Program (HEP); the importance of diagnostics given the presence of both *Plasmodium falciparum* and *P. vivax* each with distinct treatment regimens according to current national guidelines; and the instability of malaria transmission and historical pattern of recurrent epidemics. There have been important changes in four of these elements in recent years.

Geographical focus and scale: PMI in Ethiopia primarily focused on Oromia during the first three years of program support in Ethiopia. Oromia is both the largest and, by many health indicators, the most underserved regional state in Ethiopia. PMI commodity and operations support from FY 2014 funding will continue to concentrate primarily in Oromia. However, PMI support has continued to expand nationwide by filling commodity gaps including chloroquine, rectal artesunate, and injectable artesunate, and supporting planning, training, and use of strategic information. Besides strengthening these national level capacities, PMI will also continue to support the FMOH-led nationwide roll-out of Integrated Community Case Management (iCCM) with targeted support to districts in six regional states. This program is believed to have had a significant impact in reducing malaria disease-related morbidity and mortality, especially in children less than five years of age, which has greatly contributed to Ethiopia's progress towards achievement of Millennium Development Goal 4. PMI also has expanded its support for malaria laboratory strengthening activities to other regional states in cooperation with the Ethiopian Health and Nutrition Research Institute (EHNRI).

Diagnostics and the treatment of malaria and pneumonia: The HEP is a cornerstone of the FMOH's malaria control strategy. In recent years, the FMOH has refined its HEP strategy by supplying Health Extension Workers (HEWs) with multi-species rapid diagnostic tests (RDTs), that can diagnose both *P. falciparum* and *P. vivax*, and with stocks of chloroquine for the treatment of *P. vivax* (which was previously often treated with artemether-lumefantrine (AL)). Beginning in 2012, rectal artesunate has been supplied to HEWs for pre-referral treatment of severe febrile illness. In addition, HEWs have now been trained to treat suspected pneumonia cases with antibiotics such as cotrimoxazole, and to manage diarrheal illness with oral rehydration solution. These new tools are being rolled-out through iCCM and have the potential to greatly increase the HEWs' capacity for accurate differential diagnosis and correct clinical management of acute fevers at the community level.

Entomological monitoring and insecticide selection: With support from PMI, Ethiopia has greatly expanded its capacity for entomological monitoring, including testing for insecticide resistance in anopheline mosquitoes. Evidence of resistance to dichloro-diphenyl-trichloroethane (DDT) and, in some areas, to pyrethroids, prompted the FMOH to pursue a long-term insecticide resistance management strategy and to discontinue DDT after almost six decades of use as the insecticide of choice. A network of Ethiopian institutions and entomologists has been established to sustain and coordinate entomological monitoring, which will provide an evidence basis for decision making on the use and deployment of indoor residual spraying (IRS) and long-lasting insecticide treated nets (LLINs).

Epidemic threat: So-called "epidemic years," occurring every five to eight years, have been the typical pattern of malaria in Ethiopia, with the last such epidemic years occurring in 2003-2004 when more than 200 districts were affected with an estimated 41,000 deaths including 25,000 children under the age of five years. The western, central, and eastern highlands between altitudes 1,500-2,000 meters, as well as the highland-fringe areas along the Rift Valley are especially vulnerable to epidemics. Especially large malaria epidemics were documented in 1988, 1991, 1992, 1998, and 2003-2004. Population movements including seasonal migrant workers, local flooding, and famine conditions, and emerging resistance to antimalarial drugs and insecticides may also affect local communities' risks for local seasonal malaria transmission and for malaria epidemics. While no epidemics were reported in 2006 or 2007, as many as twelve district level outbreaks have been reported between 2008 and mid-2013. The apparent suppression of major malaria epidemics within the last decade is unprecedented in recent history, providing a hopeful sign that the nationally scaled up standard Roll Back Malaria (RBM) interventions are having a favorable impact on malaria control and prevention in Ethiopia. The unstable and largely unpredictable epidemiology of malaria in Ethiopia makes accurate, timely surveillance of paramount importance.

MALARIA SITUATION IN ETHIOPIA

Epidemiology

In Ethiopia, malaria transmission is largely determined by altitude and climate as affected by Indian Ocean conditions and global weather patterns, including *El Nino* and *La Nina*. Most of the malaria transmission occurs between September and December, after the main rainy season from June to August. Certain areas, largely in the western and eastern parts of the country, experience a second "minor" malaria transmission period from April to May, following a short rainy season from February to March. Five main malaria eco-epidemiological strata are recognized:

- Stable, year round, transmission in the western lowlands and river basin areas of Gambella and Benishangul-Gumuz Regional States;
- Seasonal transmission in lowland areas <1,500 meters;
- Epidemic-prone areas in highland fringes between 1,500 – 2,500 meters;
- Arid areas where malaria is only found near semi-permanent water bodies; and
- Malaria-free highland areas >2,500 meters.

Additional stratification is based on annual rainfall (Figure 1).

Figure 1. Distribution and Seasonality of Malaria in Ethiopia.

The 2007 Malaria Indicator Survey (MIS) indicated that parasite prevalence (as measured by microscopy) in Ethiopia was 0.7% and 0.3%, respectively for *P. falciparum* and *P. vivax* below 2,000 meters altitude. The 2011 MIS shows that 1.3% of all age groups were positive for malaria using microscopy and 4.5% were positive for malaria using RDTs below 2,000 meters. *P. falciparum* constituted 77% of these infections. The 2011 MIS survey demonstrated a remarkable demarcation of malaria risk at an altitude of 2,000 meters, with a thirteen-fold higher malaria prevalence at lower altitudes compared to higher elevations. There was essentially no *P. falciparum* detected by microscopy among persons surveyed within households having measured elevations above 2,000 meters in the 2011 MIS.

Burden of Clinical Malaria

Despite the low malaria parasite prevalence compared to many African countries, malaria remains the leading communicable disease seen at health facilities in Ethiopia. Historically, malaria has forced people to inhabit the less agriculturally productive highlands. Given that the country's economy is based on agriculture and peak malaria transmission coincides with the planting and harvesting season, this has placed a heavy economic burden on the country.

As stated previously, malaria is the leading cause of outpatient consultations and of health facility admissions. About 75% of the geographic area of the country has significant malaria transmission risk (defined as areas <2,000 m), with about 68% (57.3 million) of the country's total population living in these areas.

The FMOH estimates that there are about 12 million suspected malaria cases each year. The FMOH reported a total of 3,384,589 malaria cases from July 2011-June 2012, with 1,793,832 (53.0%) of these laboratory confirmed, with 1,061,242 (59.2%) *P. falciparum* and 732,590 (40.8%) *P. vivax*. Ethiopia reported 936 malaria deaths in 2011, according to the 2012 World Malaria Report.

Malaria morbidity reporting from these official FMOH surveillance sources and systems is improving, but is still substantially incomplete. PMI sponsored a microplanning survey in late 2012 to help estimate malaria morbidity and malaria commodity requirements based upon July 2011-June 2012 district level reports from all districts in Ethiopia, with essentially 100% completeness. This microplanning survey documented 11,127,705 suspected malaria cases, of which 9,255,139 (83%) were tested with microscopy or RDT; 5,522,462 malaria cases were diagnosed as malaria, including 3,649,896 laboratory confirmed and 1,872,566 probable malaria cases (which were treated without diagnostic testing). There were 2,475,337 laboratory confirmed *P. falciparum* cases, and 1,174,559 *P. vivax* cases reported. Of those who underwent diagnostic testing (9,255,139), 39% were confirmed to have malaria. From these microplanning data, an estimated 2,976,165 *P. falciparum* and 1,412,204 *P. vivax* cases would have been diagnosed had all of the 11,127,705 suspected malaria patients been laboratory tested. There were 44,696 hospitalizations for severe malaria during this time period according to the microplan reports. The higher malaria test rate (83%) in the microplan compared to FMOH surveillance estimates (53%) represents very complete microplan data collection combined with inclusion of health post data, where compliance with RDT testing by HEWs to guide treatment is apparently very high, in comparison with FMOH surveillance data from health centers and hospitals only, where microscopy services may be intermittent. It appears that the annual artemisinin-based combination therapy (ACT) requirements in Ethiopia may continue to decline well below the peak of approximately 9 million ACT treatments annually as RDTs and microscopy continue to be scaled-up especially at rural health posts, since more than half of malaria outpatients are diagnosed and treated by HEWs.

As previously mentioned, there were widespread severe malaria epidemics in 2003-2004 in Ethiopia, with an estimated 41,000 malaria deaths, including 25,000 deaths among children under five years of age in 2003. There was an apparent low point of outpatient malaria morbidity in 2007, but an estimated 30% increase in annual malaria outpatient morbidity since 2007. Ethiopian malaria surveillance data was imprecise in years prior to 2011, when most malaria cases were clinically diagnosed and malaria reporting was grossly incomplete. While no large malaria epidemics were reported in 2006 and 2007, there were several focal outbreaks reported in Southern Nations, Nationalities and People's Regional State (SNNPR), Amhara, Tigray, and Oromia in the last five years. Despite a recent apparent modest increase in outpatient malaria morbidity, annual malaria deaths in children under five years of age and malaria epidemics in Ethiopia have substantially decreased through early 2013, compared to the baseline year of 2003-2004. The FMOH's health and health related indicators report for 2010/11 shows deaths due to malaria in under five years constitute 12.6% compared to 21.1% in 2003/04. The World Health Statistics report by WHO estimated that there were 5,400 malaria deaths in Ethiopia in 2010 among Ethiopian children under five years of age, but a comprehensive analysis of all available data including recent surveillance reports suggests that the estimated number of annual malaria deaths in 2011 is 550, which is much lower for this age group.

Malaria Vectors

Anopheles arabiensis, a member of the *An. gambiae* complex, is the primary malaria vector in Ethiopia, with *An. funestus, An. pharoensis* and *An. nili* secondary vectors. The sporozoite rate for *An. arabiensis* has been recorded to be as much as 5.4%. The host-seeking behavior of *An. Arabiensis* varies, with the human blood index collected from different areas ranging between 7.7 and 100%. *An. funestus*, a mosquito that prefers to feed on humans, can be found along the swamps of Baro and Awash rivers and shores of lakes in Tana in the North and the Rift Valley area. *An. pharoensis* is widely distributed in Ethiopia and has shown high levels of insecticide resistance, but its role in malaria transmission is unclear. *An. nili* can be an important vector for malaria, particularly in Gambella Regional State. Detailed information on the basic ecology and distribution of these vectors in Ethiopia is provided in the FY 2008 MOP. However, insecticide resistance among these vectors has become an important issue, with implications for vector control strategies.

ETHIOPIA'S HEALTH SYSTEM

Ethiopia operates under a federal system of government. Administratively, the country is divided into regional states, zones, districts (*woredas*), and communities/municipalities (*kebeles*) (see Figure 2). There are about 700 districts with substantial malaria risk in Ethiopia, with an estimated at-risk population of 57.3 million people. The best available proxy for local malaria transmission risk in Ethiopia is household altitude below 2,000 meters (above sea level), since malaria is rarely transmitted at higher elevations (unless there are widespread epidemics). Many districts have variable topographical features, with some households within communities located above and other households located below 2,000 meters. Due in part to household locations at various altitudes and distances from efficient malaria vector breeding sites, malaria risk is unevenly distributed within many districts and *kebeles*.

Figure 2. Administrative Regional States and Zones of Ethiopia

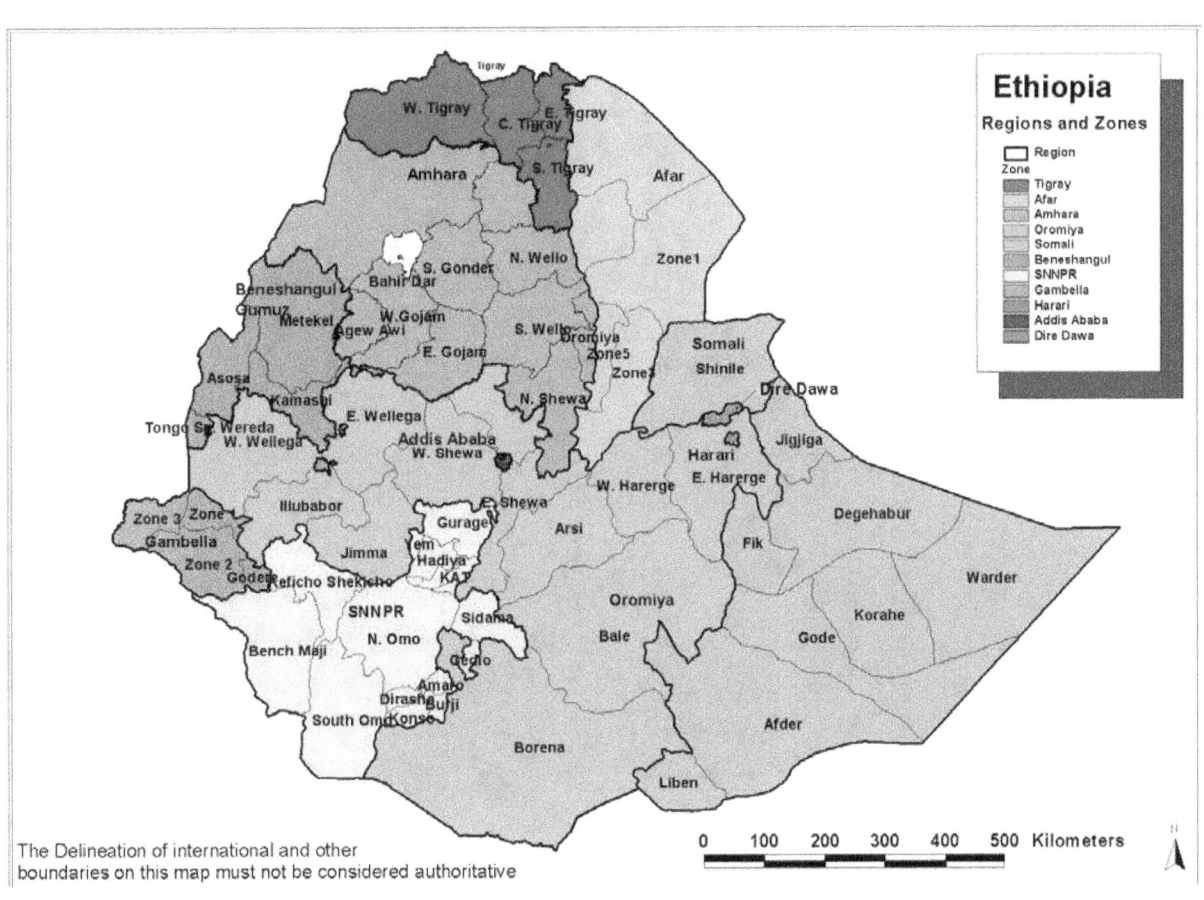

According to the 2011/2012 Health Sector Development Plan (HSDP) IV Annual Performance Report, there were a total of 125 public hospitals, 2,999 health centers, and 15,668 health posts in Ethiopia. Oromia has a population of 32 million people with 304 districts organized into 18 rural zones and also 39 'special towns' (Figure 3). According to 2010/2011 Oromia Regional

Health Bureau (ORHB) data, there are 39 hospitals, 1,098 functional health centers, and 6,052 functional health posts operated by the GoE. There are also 4 hospitals, 5 health centers and 115 health stations under other governmental organizations (e.g., teaching or armed services hospitals). In addition, there are 3 private hospitals and 1,639 private clinics, among which 1,343 are lower level, 253 are medium level, and 43 are higher level. In Oromia, the health professional to population ratio is very low with 232 physicians (0.07 per 10,000 vs. WHO standard 1:10,000), but there is better nurse coverage with 9,757 nurses (3:10,000 vs. WHO standard 2:10,000). There are 12,875 rural health extension workers and 692 Health Officers. There are a total of 3,207 available hospital beds (GoE 2,867 and non-governmental organization 340 hospital beds) with a bed-to-population ratio of 1:9,153 (WHO standard 1:3,000).

As in the rest of the country, the health care service delivery system in Oromia has been re-organized into a three-tier system. The lowest tier is known as the 'Primary Health Care Unit', which is composed of one district hospital (covering 60,000-100,000 people), health centers (1 per 25,000 people) and their satellite health posts (1 per 5,000 people). The second tier is the 'General Hospital', covering catchment population of 1-1.5 million people and the third is the 'specialized hospital', covering a population of 3.5 to 5 million people.

Figure 3. Administrative Zones and Districts of Oromia Regional State

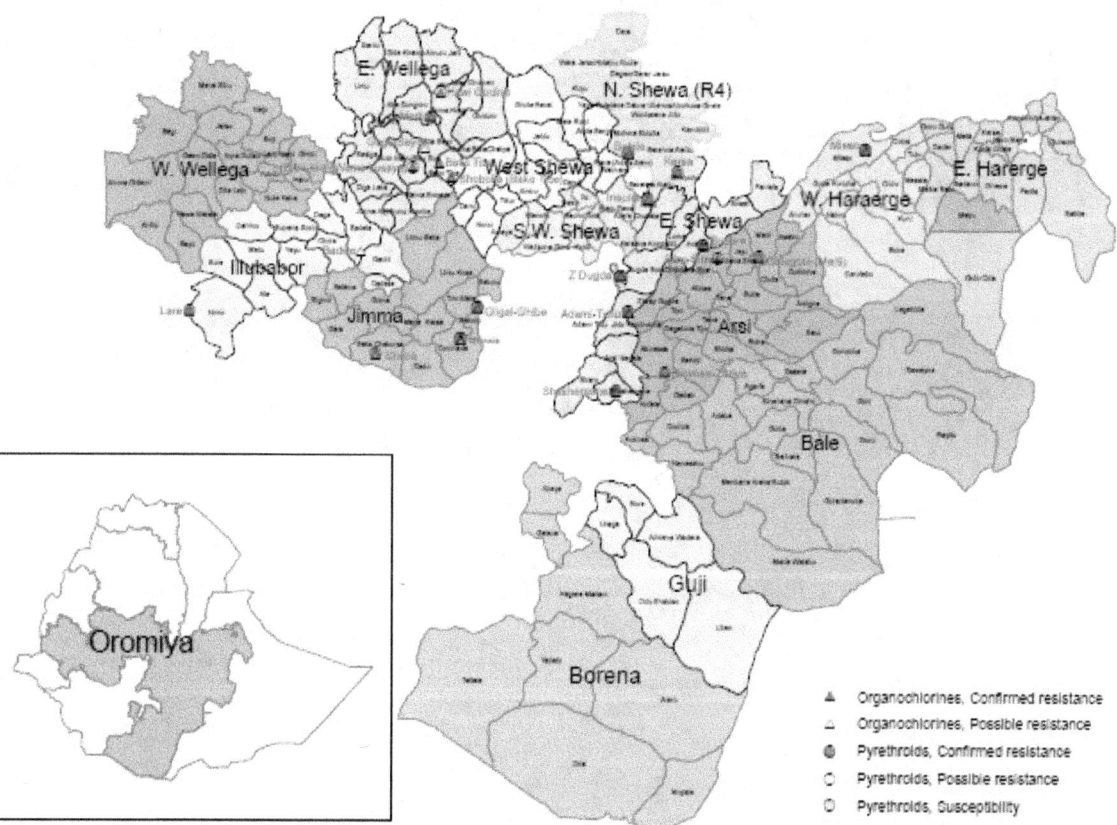

16

The typical health post is staffed by two HEWs delivering 16 selected health packages, including one health package on malaria [http://cnhde.ei.columbia.edu/training/index.html]. HEWs are paid FMOH staff; they undergo a one-year training after a high school diploma, and usually originate from the communities they serve. The HEWs focus on preventive services, however, they also provide curative healthcare services for malaria, pneumonia, and diarrhea using the iCCM approach of evidence-based diagnostic and treatment algorithms. For malaria, HEWs have been trained to confirm and report malaria diagnoses among clinically evaluated acutely ill patients using malaria multispecies RDTs. Severe malaria cases are to be referred to the next appropriate health facility, with initial stabilization with rectal artesunate. The HEWs are encouraged to consider other diagnostic possibilities for patients who test negative by malaria RDT, and to avoid empiric treatment with antimalarials when malaria RDTs are available. The HEWs are also expected to supervise seasonal activities, including social behavior change communication (SBCC) and mass vaccination campaigns, participate in surveys and a range of other community health activities. Additionally, HEWs have become more directly involved in supervising IRS spray teams and door-to-door mobilization for IRS. The FMOH envisages decentralizing IRS operations to the primary health care unit, where HEWs would be responsible for supervising the operations in their catchment area (*kebele*). Nevertheless, this approach has not been fully developed and there are concerns that this may result in a drop in the quality of spray operations, substandard environmental compliance, and use of insecticide for unintended purposes.

The health center provides comprehensive primary health care services and backup to the health posts by accepting referral cases, while district and general hospitals provide secondary health care. Health centers typically can provide inpatient services for up to two malaria patients, and they are equipped with injectable artesunate for severe malaria treatment. In Oromia, hospitals in Adama, Nekemte, Asella, Mettu, and Ambo serve as general referral hospitals. Jimma Hospital, under the Ministry of Education, is providing tertiary level health care for the city of Jimma and the surrounding population.

ETHIOPIA'S MALARIA CONTROL STRATEGY

Under the framework of HSDP IV, 2011-2015, Ethiopia developed a five-year National Strategic Plan for Malaria Prevention, Control and Elimination (2011 – 2015). This strategic plan was developed following the 2007 MIS, as well as the discussions and recommendations following a consultative meeting held in Adama, Ethiopia, in March 2009 with key in-country and international malaria stakeholders. The HSDP and the national strategic plan are in line with RBM partnership objectives. The following goals and objectives are set out in the five-year strategic plan:

Goals

- By 2015, achieve malaria elimination within specific geographical areas with historically low malaria transmission; and
- By 2015, achieve zero deaths due to malaria in the remaining areas with malaria transmission.

Overall objective

The objective of the National Strategic Plan for Malaria Prevention and Control 2011 – 2015 is to consolidate the achievements of the 2006 – 2010 strategic plan and sustain its impact.

Specific objectives

- 100% of suspected malaria cases are diagnosed using RDTs and/or microscopy within 24 hours of fever onset;
- 100% of positive malaria diagnoses are treated according to national guidelines;
- 100% of households in malarious areas own, on average, two LLINs;
- At least 80% of people at risk of malaria use LLINs;
- IRS coverage is increased and maintained to 90% of households in IRS-targeted areas;
- 100% of health posts in malarious *kebeles* provide the full malaria prevention and treatment package, including outreach services; and
- To achieve a high quality, broadly-based malaria infection detection, investigation and response surveillance system to further reduce malaria transmission.

In the new strategic plan, community empowerment and social mobilization are given top priority among malaria control strategies, based on the results of the 2007 MIS which showed substantial differences between the coverage and utilization of key malaria interventions by the populations at risk of malaria. Similarly, malaria diagnosis, case management, disease surveillance and epidemic control are geared to serve Ethiopia's goal of shrinking malaria endemic areas by 2015 and country-wide elimination by 2020. Accordingly, all malaria diagnosis is to be based on diagnostic testing, either by microscopy or RDTs, and treatment of malaria cases is to be guided by the result of the diagnosis. Surveillance will focus primarily on individual cases to identify the sources of infection and to limit further transmission.

PMI provided technical assistance in 2012 to the FMOH to update the Ethiopian National Guidelines for malaria diagnosis and treatment, vector control, and malaria epidemic detection and response, which are now available on the FMOH website under "important documents" by web-searching "national malaria guidelines Ethiopia."

INTEGRATION, COLLABORATION AND COORDINATION

Maternal, Neonatal and Child Health, Family Planning, Reproductive Health

Following the first National Family Fertility Survey conducted in 1990, the USG started supporting the delivery of key maternal, neonatal and child health (MNCH), family planning, and nutrition services at the community level including expanded immunization, family planning, essential nutrition actions, malaria prevention, control and case management, promotion of antenatal care (ANC), and water, sanitation and hygiene. These interventions are delivered through health centers, health posts, and households and focus on rural, peri-urban, and hard-to-reach populations. To date, the program has trained over 60,000 community health volunteers, provided assistance to over 13,000 HEWs, and has reached over 32 million people (35% of the Ethiopian population) in 301 districts in six of the country's nine regional states. Under the Feed the Future Initiative, the USG will also continue to integrate health, agriculture, and humanitarian assistance and livelihood sector platforms to maximize impact on nutrition.

Most of PMI support to these activities is being implemented through partners supporting the rural HEWs and the recently scaled up Health Development Army at community levels with a multi-agency collaborative approach using GHI and United States Agency for International Development (USAID) processes and structures. PMI uses this platform to reach the most at-risk communities in malaria diagnosis and treatment, epidemic detection and response, and also to promote best practices in malaria case management by HEWs at health posts, including use of iCCM clinical algorithms.

PEPFAR, GHI, and other USG Programs

PMI is working with PEPFAR within the GHI framework through USAID and Centers for Disease Control and Prevention (CDC) structures, to harmonize the Ethiopia FY 2014 Country Operational Plan, with the USAID Health team's Operational Plan for tuberculosis and population health to ensure the respective plans complement and strengthen each other. Thus, currently approximately 20% of PMI's budget is allocated to so-called 'wrap around' activities with PEPFAR, i.e., either through co-funding of an award or by leveraging resources that have been established through previous PEPFAR support (e.g., laboratory infrastructure strengthening overlapping with HIV and tuberculosis diagnosis, malaria SBCC harmonization with other health messages, pharmacy system and supply chain strengthening). PMI also has important cooperative malaria bed net hang up projects with U.S. Department of Defense Combined Joint Task Force-Horn of Africa (CJTF-HOA) and other malaria prevention projects with Peace Corps and CDC (i.e., Field Epidemiology and Laboratory Training Program (FELTP)) within the GHI context.

Neglected Tropical Diseases

Several neglected tropical diseases (NTDs) are prevalent in Ethiopia, including soil-transmitted helminths, filariasis, leishmaniasis, onchocerciasis, schistosomiasis, and trachoma. The FMOH and other in-country stakeholders have detailed information concerning some of these NTDs, but data for other NTDs is limited (e.g., filariasis and schistosomiasis). Only trachoma and onchocerciasis have large-scale intervention programs in Ethiopia, with mass drug administration campaigns using azithromycin and ivermectin, respectively. For those areas where malaria, filariasis and leishmaniasis occur, it is likely that the malaria vector control interventions of IRS and LLINs will also have a beneficial impact on other vector-borne diseases.

PMI also supported the development of a malaria risk map for Oromia and SNNPR regional states using data from school-based malaria surveys. Leveraging additional funding support from the Wellcome Trust, school children were surveyed for helminths. Continued efforts are needed to reduce anemia prevalence in children, both by controlling malaria and soil-transmitted helminths.

PMI in-country staff is assisting the FMOH in finalizing a National Neglected Tropical Disease Strategy as well as supporting the FMOH in coordination and integration of malaria activities with activities planned under the NTD strategy. Additional USAID-funded NTD related activities are in the planning phase under the leadership of the Health team at USAID/Ethiopia. It is expected that PMI/Ethiopia will continue to play a supportive role in these efforts by providing technical assistance as needed, but not to include PMI funding for NTD-specific activities.

Coordination with other Partners

The Malaria Control Support Team (MCST) provides coordinated malaria technical support to the national and regional programs and is comprised of members of the FMOH, donor and international organizations, governmental and non-governmental organizations, and academia. The primary task of the MCST is to support the FMOH and regional health bureaus (RHBs) through ongoing technical assistance, resource mobilization, and support to epidemic preparedness and response. The MCST provides a common forum to share duties and responsibilities, avoid duplication and discuss priorities. PMI has been a member of the MCST since 2008.

Part of the MCST is the Technical Advisory Committee (TAC), which includes the main malaria stakeholders in the country, i.e., FMOH, The Carter Center, Malaria Control and Evaluation Partnership in Africa (MACEPA), Malaria Consortium, PMI, UNICEF, WHO, etc. PMI is also a member of the TAC representing a technical core of the MCST which advises the FMOH on policy and program implementation issues, providing technical assistance on an ad hoc basis, and assisting with malaria program integration issues.

PMI has also been instrumental in the development and finalization of five Global Fund proposals (Round 7, 8 and 10, Round 2 Rolling Continuation Channel, and recent Transitional Funding Mechanism) as well as the development and updating of in-country guidelines and strategies. Experts from the Global Fund were consulted in early 2013 to help develop this FY 2014 MOP document.

In addition, PMI is supporting coordination of malaria research stakeholders, academia and FMOH to fill the gap between the implementation of emerging malaria knowledge and research and the adoption of best malaria practices by researchers, practitioners, policymakers, and organizations involved in the prevention and control of the disease. Resolving this gap would serve to increase the benefits of quality research to improve prevention and control, and avoid duplication of efforts and waste of resources.

PMI GOALS, TARGETS AND INDICATORS

Under the GHI, the goal of PMI is to reduce the burden of malaria (morbidity and mortality) by 70% compared to baseline levels in the initial PMI countries. Specifically, the reduction of malaria deaths among children under five years of age from a baseline of 2000-2004 is a major PMI goal while working in partnership with FMOH and many other partners. By 2015, PMI will have assisted the Oromia Regional State and the FMOH to achieve the following targets in populations at risk for malaria and targeted by activities supported by PMI:

- >90% of households with a pregnant woman and/or children <5 years of age will own at least one ITN;
- 85% of children <5 years of age will have slept under an ITN the previous night;
- 85% of pregnant women will have slept under an ITN the previous night;
- 85% of houses in geographic areas targeted for IRS will have been sprayed;
- 85% of pregnant women and children <5 years of age will have slept under an ITN the previous night or in a house that has been sprayed with IRS in the last 12 months (note, because of the highly seasonal transmission of malaria in Ethiopia, one spray round per year is thought to be enough to protect the community); and
- 85% of government health facilities have ACTs available for treatment of uncomplicated malaria.

PROGRESS ON COVERAGE AND IMPACT INDICATORS

Malaria Indicator Survey (MIS) 2007 and 2011

The 2007 and 2011 MIS assessed key malaria interventions, treatment-seeking behavior, anemia prevalence in children less than five years of age, malaria prevalence in all age groups, malaria knowledge among women, and indicators of socioeconomic status. PMI provided technical and financial support to over-sample Oromia Regional State to provide a regionally representative baseline and follow-up for PMI activities. For both respective surveys, field work was carried out from October to December during the high transmission season. The survey results were stratified by regional states and altitude (with communities <2,000 meters considered 'malarious'), and thus designated for FMOH targeting.

Table 1. Key Malaria Indicators Reported in DHS 2005, MIS 2007 and MIS 2011

Indicator	DHS 2005 National	MIS 2007 National (< 2,000 m)	MIS 2007 National (≤ 2,500 m)	MIS 2007 Oromia (≤ 2,500 m)	MIS2011 National <2000m	MIS2011 Oromia <2000m
Percent households with at least one LLIN	3.4	65.3	53.1	41	54.8	43.7
Percent households with more than one LLIN	-	36.6	29.5	21.4	23.6	17.3
Percent children < 5 years of age sleeping under an LLIN the previous night	1.6	41.5	33.1	24.3	38.0	26.5
Percent pregnant women sleeping under an LLIN the previous night	1.1	42.7	35.2	25.6	34.7	26.7
Percent households reporting indoor residual spraying in the past 12 months	2.3	20.0	14.2	12.5	46.6	43.0
Percentage of households protected by at least one LLIN and/or IRS					71.7	63.7
Percent children < 5 years of age with fever in past two weeks	-	24.0	22.3	21.5	19.7	15.4
Percent children with fever who took antimalarial drugs	0.7	11.9	9.5	6.6	32.6	38.8
Percent who took an antimalarial drug same or next day	-	4.8	3.9	1.3	8.5	13.8
Percent children with fever who sought treatment from facility/provider same/next day	-	16.3	15.4	16.4	51.3	59.5
Malaria prevalence by microscopy *P. falciparum* (%)	-	0.7	0.5	0.1	1.0	0.2
Malaria prevalence by microscopy *P. vivax* (%)	-	0.3	0.2	0.2	0.3	0.3

Table 2. Malaria Knowledge among Eligible Women Age 15-49 years

Survey	Region	Percent who have heard of malaria	Percent who recognize fever as symptom	Percent who report mosquito bite as cause	Percent who report nets for prevention
MIS 2007	National (< 2000 m)	79.5	50.8	41.1	38.2
	National (≤ 2500 m)	74.6	44.4	35.8	32.8
	Oromia (≤ 2500 m)	68.8	31.6	32.0	22.6
MIS 2011	National (<2000m)	71.3	76.0	71.2	63.4
	Oromia (<2000m)	68.7	71.3	73.2	65.5

Compared to the Demographic and Health Survey (DHS) conducted in 2005, results from the MIS 2007 reflect the significant effort of the FMOH-led scale-up of malaria prevention and control interventions, with substantial increases in ITN ownership and use, as well as malaria knowledge. The 2011 MIS did not show an improvement in LLIN ownership or use from MIS 2007, but those seeking treatment for fevers within 24 hours and women's malaria knowledge were markedly improved. Tables 1 and 2 report national data for areas <2,000m and <2,500m; whereas, data reported for Oromia includes all areas ≤ 2,500m in 2007 and <2,000m in 2011).

Both the 2007 and 2011 MIS showed the gaps in the scale-up of malaria interventions, clearly indicating needs for better targeting of LLIN distributions and a comprehensive SBCC approach to (i) maximize use of ITNs; (ii) maximize the efforts made in scaling-up IRS activities (e.g., by reducing refusal rates of households to be sprayed and decreasing the practice of replastering walls after IRS); and (iii) continue to increase access to malaria case management services.

Hospital Surveys 2007 – 2010

In 2007, with the support of WHO, the FMOH carried out a hospital survey in a stratified convenience sample of 13 hospitals in Afar, Amhara, Oromia, and Tigray. The main impact indicators were percentage change in number of in-patient malaria cases, in-patient malaria deaths and laboratory-confirmed out-patient cases in children < 5 and ≥ 5 years old prior to 2001–2005/6 and after 2007 (i.e., after the nationwide implementation of LLINs and ACTs).

Comparing 2007 against the average of 2001–2006, declines of 73% for children < 5 years old in inpatient malaria cases, 62% for inpatient malaria deaths, and 85% for outpatient laboratory-confirmed cases were observed. Adjusting for pre-intervention trends, the estimated declines in the two age groups ranged from 3% to 91% across the malaria indicators and age groups for which statistical testing was possible. For inpatient deaths in children under five years of age, too few data points were available to allow statistical testing. In comparison, non-malaria out-patient cases and in-patient cases and deaths were higher (by 1% to 45%) in 2007 compared to the average of 2001–2006, except for inpatient deaths which declined by 13% for those <5 years and 31% for those ≥ 5 years of age. After adjustment for trends over 2001–2006, non-malaria inpatient cases declined significantly, ranging from 11–25%, while outpatient cases increased in children <5 years of age, but decreased in the age group ≥ 5 years of age. For in-patient deaths, no significant changes were apparent in 2007, when adjusting for prior time trends.

Although the findings were encouraging, their relevance for the overall monitoring of national malaria intervention efforts was limited due to a number of factors, including the survey's small sample size and the exclusion of health centers and health posts, where most malaria cases are being diagnosed and treated. Other investigators recently estimated that among children less than five years of age in Ethiopia, 376,922 and 277,186 deaths from all causes, and 7,743 and 4,514 malaria deaths occurred in years 2000 and 2010, respectively.

Epidemic Detection Sites 2010 – 2013

Beginning in March 2010, PMI assisted ORHB to fully scale up support to malaria epidemic detection sites (*see also M&E section*) within ten malarious districts in Oromia Regional State. These ten epidemic detection sites comprise of health centers and their satellite community-level health posts, serving a combined catchment area of approximately 450,000 people and featuring weekly reporting of laboratory confirmed malaria morbidity via weekly text messages from 83 health facilities.

During the initial surveillance interval of 37 months since the system was established, 338,186 patients attended health services at these sites through March 2013. Of these, 141,575 patients were tested for malaria, and 35,618 (25%) of these had a confirmatory diagnosis for either mixed or *P. falciparum* (~46%) or *P. vivax* (~54%) only. The overall incidence of hospitalizations for severe malaria was 99/35,618 (0.3%) among those with confirmed malaria; two deaths due to malaria were reported from these ten sites within the last three years. Four district level malaria epidemics were detected (using standard WHO criteria): two due to *P. falciparum* and two due to *P. vivax*. An epidemic of relapsing fever due to louse-borne borreliosis was also detected by this surveillance system. This epidemic detection system also helped to promptly identify and mitigate shortages of malaria commodities such as antimalarial medicines and laboratory reagents.

At one of the ten districts, a *P. falciparum* epidemic lasted about nine months, causing one death and 62 hospitalizations. The outbreak continued despite prompt detection, maintenance of adequate diagnostic and treatment capacities, and three rounds of IRS. After a special investigation revealed very low LLIN coverage in the district and evidence of vector insecticide resistance, the malaria outbreak waned after PMI helped organize a bed net hang-up, and keep-up campaign to facilitate distribution and proper use of PMI nets jointly with CJTF-HOA and an implementing partner specializing in SBCC.

CHALLENGES, OPPORTUNITIES AND THREATS

Challenges

Programmatic challenges in malaria prevention and control include human resources gaps including shortages of appropriately educated and trained health professionals within malaria programs in districts, RHBs, and at the FMOH, and high staff turnover. PMI supports the FELTP that is designed to educate and train epidemiologists and laboratory personnel supporting malaria programs in Ethiopia. PMI also supports WHO district-level malaria program trainings, integrated refresher trainings and iCCM trainings per FMOH request.

Supply chain issues are an ongoing challenge. Ethiopia is a large country, with many remote areas that are far from major roads, providing challenges to delivering essential commodities to districts and to health centers. Even more challenging is delivering commodities to health posts and households in remote rural areas within districts where access is especially difficult during the rainy seasons. Information management systems to detect malaria commodity shortages and stockouts need strengthening.

Opportunities

The FMOH is committed to malaria prevention and control, giving high priority to health interventions that are also supported by PMI. There is especially high political commitment for the HEP. This is an important opportunity for malaria prevention and control since the HEP supports diagnostic testing and treatment for malaria, stabilization and referral of severe cases (including the use of rectal artesunate), LLIN distribution, and epidemic detection and response. Social behavior change communication activities are delegated increasingly to the HEP and to the new Health Development Army that augments activities of HEWs in rural communities. Diverse elements of the Ethiopian public health system, academia, NGOs, and many other malaria stakeholders are committed to support the FMOH's effort in malaria prevention and control. The FMOH consults the Malaria Control Support Team's TAC and its sub committees for most technical issues. The TAC had been involved in helping to draft proposals for Global Fund grants and helping to ensure that PMI's support to FMOH integrates well with Global Fund malaria support in Ethiopia.

PMI has several implementing partners, especially UNICEF, that are capable of procuring, importing, and distributing malaria commodities in a manner that harmonizes with FMOH's similar processes for Global Fund procurements. The Pharmaceutical Funding and Supply Agency (PFSA) has been strengthened by several years of PEPFAR support, and is actively supported by PMI's supply chain partners. Another PMI implementing partner has supported the Food, Medicine and Healthcare Administration and Control Authority (FMHACA) in assessing and maintaining the quality of antimalarial drugs. PMI expects to work more closely in the future with PFSA through various supply chain partners to meet the FMOH malaria program needs.

Threats

Variable weather conditions, including *El Nino* and *La Nina*, that affect seasonal rains, and global warming trends may fuel malaria vector proliferation with resulting focal and widespread malaria epidemics, and may also create famines and population migrations. In response, PMI supports a malaria epidemic detection system in ten districts within Oromia Regional State using weekly SMS reporting. The system is expected to expand to 40 districts under EHNRI supervision to supplement surveillance provided the Public Health Emergency Management (PHEM) system and HMIS. PMI also supports the FELTP designed to investigate and help mitigate possible malaria outbreaks.

Currently standard malaria treatment includes AL for *P. falciparum* and chloroquine for *P. vivax* infections. In Southeast Asia, antimalarial drug resistance has been well documented for these medicines. It is important to continue to document *in vivo* drug efficacy of these medicines and to provide an evidence basis for use of appropriate medicines for the respective infecting malaria species according to a laboratory-based diagnosis. PMI's promotion of best practices in malaria care and treatment such as assisting with drafting of the recently updated FMOH malaria diagnosis and treatment guidelines should help to reduce overuse of antimalarial medicines and delay the onset of antimalarial drug resistance.

Well-documented insecticide resistance already threatens the effectiveness of IRS and makes such operations increasingly costly. Indoor residual spraying requires precise targeting to ensure that spraying will be effective and scarce resources are not wasted. There are concerns that increasing pyrethroid (deltamethrin) resistance will reduce effectiveness of both IRS and LLINs. Alternative insecticides to pyrethroids require less convenient timing of IRS application, and are more costly to keep the existing coverage. Proper handling, storage, and disposal of unused insecticides such as DDT pose occupational health, environmental impact and logistical challenges. PMI supports ongoing monitoring of the emerging insecticide resistance situation to assist the FMOH, and continues to promote best practices in insecticide use.

PMI SUPPORT STRATEGY

PMI's support strategy for Ethiopia has evolved since PMI began its activities in FY 2008. Originally, support was focused primarily on Oromia Regional State. Since 2011, PMI has expanded its support in a number of areas beyond Oromia, providing technical assistance to national structures, and technical and programmatic support and commodities to other Regional States.

Support activities continued to be focused on scaling up LLINs, IRS, and improved case management, along with supportive activities such as SBCC, strengthening supply chain management and strategic information (i.e., surveillance, epidemic detection, and commodities microplanning).

PMI's support to Ethiopia is in line with GoE's HSDP (2011-2015) and National Strategic Plan for Malaria Prevention and Control (2011 – 2015). Funding is targeted to fill gaps in activities that are not already supported by the FMOH, Global Fund, or other donors. PMI support also has been flexible and responsive to the FMOH's evolving needs, and has sometimes reprogrammed resources to provide critical malaria commodities and has developed and sustained other core competencies and capacities that are needed by FMOH but that are not optimally supported by other funding agencies or the GoE. Additionally, PMI has provided considerable technical support and expertise for FMOH that is enriched with connectivity to malaria subject matter experts at CDC/Atlanta, USAID/Washington and academic and development partners worldwide.

OPERATIONAL PLAN

INSECTICIDE-TREATED NETS (ITNs)

NMCP/PMI Objectives

The Ethiopia National Malaria Strategic Plan recognizes use of LLINs as a cornerstone for malaria disease prevention in the country. The key strategy used by the country is a rolling periodic (every three years) free distribution of LLINs to all population groups living in endemic, high and moderate malaria risk areas of Ethiopia. Two LLINs per household was used as an operational guideline until 2011. That policy was then changed and, currently, Ethiopia aims to achieve universal coverage by distributing one LLIN per 1.8 persons through mass, free distribution campaigns at the community level through the HEWs and/or health facilities. Ethiopia has distributed about 52 million LLINs since 2005. Usually, ITNs are distributed by periodic mass campaigns that occur about every three years in rotation using microplanning data. The FMOH generally does not support routine ITN distribution by ANC or EPI clinics.

Table 3: LLIN distribution by different programs in Ethiopia (2005-2012)

Year	UNICEF	GF 2	GF 5	GF 8	WB	Carter Center	PSI	MDG	PMI	Total ITNs
2005	1,223,957	2,500,000	-		-	-	100,000			3,823,957
2006	354,750	3,825,500	-		-	-	300,000			4,480,250
2007	1,750,000	-	3,348,168		3,500,000	3,000,000	200,000			11,798,168
2008		-	778,423		1,600,000	-	-			2,378,423
2009		-	2,171,528		1,685,000	-	-		559,500	4,416,028
2010	180,000	-	11,350,000		114,600	5,958,897	-		1,000,000	18,603,497
2011	25,000	-	-	-	-	-	-	859,162	1,845,000	2,729,162
2012		-	-	1,000,000	-	-	-		2,540,000	3,540,000
Total	3,533,707	6,325,500	17,648,119	1,000,000	6,899,600	8,958,897	600,000	859,162	5,944,500	51,769,485

The recent MIS showed significant improvements in LLIN household ownership in malaria risk areas from 3.4% in 2005 (DHS 2005) to 65% in 2007 and 55% in 2011 (MIS 2007, 2011). The proportion of children under five year of age who used an LLIN the previous night living below 2,000 meters increased from 1.6% in 2005 (DHS) to 42% in 2007 and 38% in 2011.

Progress During the Last 12 Months

Between FY 2008 and FY 2012, PMI procured a total of 5.9 million LLINs, which were distributed to malaria risk communities under universal coverage approach primarily through the HEWs in Oromia Regional State. Distribution of LLINs was based on an Oromia-wide microplan developed by PMI in collaboration with the ORHB.

The microplanning exercise that PMI supported includes district and *kebele*-level data on the number of malaria cases and key malaria commodities including RDTs, ACTs, chloroquine, and LLINs. For LLINs, each annual microplanning meeting compiles records of the number of LLINs previously distributed within the last three years, and documents LLINs that were more than three years old and thus need to be replaced. The microplan estimates the 12-month need and gap of LLINs based on district-level sub-populations with malaria risk (generally by *kebele*), malaria morbidity, and LLIN data.

In addition to replacement of LLINs, the number of "gap filling" nets was calculated by quantifying the number of new households (resulting from population growth rates) and malaria affected households that never received nets in previous distributions. The microplanning process has now been adopted by other Regional States and has helped streamline and coordinate the commodity procurement and distribution process as well as allowing for tracking and prioritization of commodity distributions.

PMI carried out LLIN enhanced hang-up activities in 17 districts, involving a total of 399,100 LLINs since 2010 with support from CJTF-HOA, Peace Corps, and ORHB. From this total, the U.S. military's CJTF-HOA was involved in hang-up assist projects for 276,900 LLINs within 11 districts. Between June 2012 and June 2013, enhanced hang-up campaigns were conducted by PMI in ten districts, resulting in the hang-up of over 173,000 LLINs. In July 2010 and in March

2012, PMI helped distribute and hang nets in two districts in the midst of focal malaria epidemics, and in both cases, the malaria upsurge resolved promptly.

In late 2012, microplanning identified a 21.8 million LLIN gap for 2013. The FMOH planned to use Global Fund Round 8 Phase 2 and transitional funding mechanism (TFM) funding to procure 15.5 million nets in 2013 while PMI planned to contribute a total of 5.7 million LLINs (1.2 million via MOP FY 2011 and 4.5 million via MOP FY 2012 including recent reprogramming) to cover 93% of the required nets in 2013. As of July 2013, 1.2 million LLINs had been procured through PMI and already delivered to Oromia Regional State; another 3.5 million nets had been procured through PMI but not yet delivered; and 1 million nets are pending procurement.

Challenges, Opportunities and Threats

To date, PMI-procured LLINs were distributed to the high malaria burden districts in Oromia Regional State. Some of the local districts lack operational funds to transport these nets to health posts and households. PMI funding to reimburse selected districts for distribution costs should improve distribution and reduce the risk of diversion.

LLIN Gap Analysis

Table 4: Oromia and National LLIN Gap Analysis 2013-2015

Description	2013	2014		2015	
	National	Oromia	National	Oromia	National
Population at risk (based on microplan FY 2013 considering population growth at 2.9%)	56,881,139	20,680,850	58,530,692	21,280,595	60,228,082
Operational coverage 100% of at risk population	100%	100%	100%	100%	100%
Total LLINs programmatic needed at all times (1 LLIN for 1.8 people)	31,600,633	11,489,361	33,688,733	11,822,553	33,460,046
Nets <3years: for 2013 (2011+2012), for 2014 (2012+213) and for 2015 (2013+2014)	10,926,488	9,633,229	26,124,789	8,949,361	25,788,593
Nets gaps from previous year that not addressed			1,171,682		777,814
Nets to be replaced	20,674,145	1,856,132	7,563,944	2,873,192	8,449,267
Nets Available from GFR8-II and TFM	13,802,463		2,986,130		Not known yet
Nets Available from PMI	5,700,000		3,800,000		2,100,000
Total nets available/funded	19,502,463		6,786,130		2,100,000
Nets <3 years + Available	30,428,951		32,910,919		27,888,593
Nets to be replaced - Nets available	1,171,682		777,814		6,349,267
Remaining gap	**1,171,682**		**777,814**		**6,349,267**

Plans and Justification

PMI supports the FMOH policy and distribution of LLINs to the most at-risk communities in Oromia Regional State. In addition to the LLIN procurement and distribution, PMI in collaboration with FMOH and other in-country stakeholders are currently assisting with the national microplanning process for LLIN needs assessment and plans for distribution. The FMOH requested via the Global Fund TFM grant application for 87% LLIN coverage of the at-risk population assuming 1.8 nets per person in 2013, replacing LLINs after three years. However, given the poor baseline coverage from MIS 2011, mis-targeting, etc., it is more realistic to plan for 100% coverage. In earlier FMOH grant applications, either two LLIN nets per household (averaging five persons) or one net per two persons had been requested. That policy was then changed to one LLIN per 1.8 persons. On the basis of this new strategy of 1 LLIN per 1.8 persons, the total number of nets needed per specified time will be the total population at risk divided by 1.8.

Proposed Activities with FY 2014 Funding ($8,791,600):

• **Procurement and distribution of LLINs to districts ($8,491,600):** Due to the pressing need to cover the LLIN gap, PMI will increase its support for procurement and distribution of 2.1 million LLINs to high malaria transmission areas in Oromia Regional State. The LLINs will be delivered to the district level and distributed free to communities mainly through HEWs, and in some occasions through NGOs.

• **LLIN distribution from districts to health posts/communities ($300,000):** PMI will assist some selected hard-to-reach districts to transport LLINs from district to health post and communities, at approximately $0.15/net. These districts/locations will be selected following discussions with ORHB and LLIN distribution partners. All activities will be coordinated with local authorities in order to ensure that engagement of targeted districts is maximized.

INDOOR RESIDUAL SPRAYING (IRS)

NMCP/PMI Objectives

Indoor residual spraying was first implemented in Ethiopia in the mid-1960s and has remained a key component of the national malaria prevention and control strategy since that time. In the current National Strategic Plan for Malaria Prevention and Control in Ethiopia (NSP 2011 – 2015), IRS is given high priority as a main component of vector control. The FMOH's IRS objective is "to increase and maintain IRS coverage to 90% of households in IRS-targeted areas." The targeted areas include high malaria burden areas, epidemic-prone areas, development projects, and malaria-affected communities with low access to the health care system. Specific

IRS-targeted communities (*kebeles*) are selected based on malaria case loads, altitude, presence of nearby anopheline breeding sites, agriculture and water development practices, epidemic records, and other economic or social factors (settlements, etc.). The selection of communities for IRS is refined every year and the same communities are often repeatedly selected for IRS because of continued high numbers of malaria cases or other factors conducive to high malaria transmission. Malaria transmission in Ethiopia is seasonal, lasting for about three months, mostly peaking after the main rainy season. Depending on the residual life of the insecticide used and timing of spray operations, one spray round per year could give the required protection against malaria.

Progress During the Last 12 Months

Ethiopia's spray program has expanded significantly since PMI began support for IRS in 2008, reaching a peak of 858,657 structures sprayed in 2011 (Figure 4). Since 2008, PMI provided targeted IRS to *kebeles* in PMI-supported districts according to the National Guidelines, which target the highest burden *kebeles* in targeted districts. Not all malarious *kebeles* in a specific district are targeted for IRS spraying. In FY 2008/09, DDT was sprayed in PMI-supported districts, while the pyrethroid deltamethrin was used in 2010. As per FMOH guidance, in 2011 and 2012 both deltamethrin and bendiocarb were used. PMI is supporting spraying with carbamate (i.e. bendiocarb) insecticides for all PMI-supported districts in 2013.

In 2012, PMI provided two levels of support to IRS operations in 60 districts in ten zones of Oromia Regional State; 24 districts were graduated and received minimal support, while 36 districts received full PMI support. This process of graduation was began in 2011 in 24 districts that had already received PMI support for two or more years and were considered to have sufficient capacity to assume greater financial and technical responsibility for the spray program. By 2012, these 24 districts were considered fully graduated and only received minimal support for microplanning, supportive supervision, and the provision of IRS equipment to fill gaps. The bulk of IRS-related financial and programmatic support was taken over by the districts. In contrast, 36 districts received full financial and technical support from PMI. Given the limited support provided to the 24 graduated districts, PMI only reports out on the 36 districts that received full PMI support.

Figure 4: IRS Results in PMI Supported Districts, Oromia Regional State, Ethiopia, 2008 – 2012

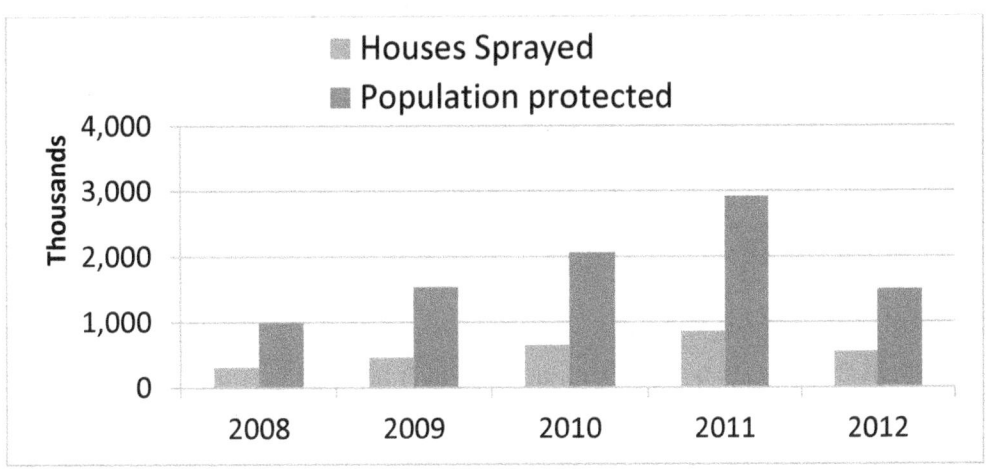

The rationale for this graduation approach is that as districts build capacity to undertake IRS operations, they can sustain the practice with less assistance and the funds saved will be used to provide greater support to IRS in new districts. According to a 2012 IRS assessment, all 24 graduated districts have conducted IRS operations with support from the government and local NGOs, covering 428,459 structures, which represents over 82% coverage in the targeted communities. As a result, these "graduated" districts will continue receiving only minimal PMI support in the future, including microplanning consultations, a limited supply of equipment, and technical assistance.

In 2012, resistance to the district graduation approach was observed in various forms. One major impediment was due to delays the district health offices faced in securing government funds for IRS operations. While the overall effectiveness of the graduation process needs further discussion and analysis, it does appear to be successful given the large amount of structures that were sprayed by the government in the 24 graduated districts.

In 2012, PMI's spray program in 36 districts achieved a 98.8% coverage rate, resulting in 547,421 sprayed structures and the protection of 1,506,273 people. Indoor residual spraying operations were conducted in two rounds in 2012, as was done in 2011. The first spray round occurred from June to early August 2012 using pyrethroids (deltamethrin) in 19 districts and the second spray round occurred from late August to early October 2012 in 17 districts, using carbamates (bendiocarb). The difference in the spray timing is due to differences in the residual life of these two insecticides. PMI supported spraying quality assurance tests in two IRS operation districts. Test results for bendiocarb on wild vector mosquitoes showed 100% mortality one month after spraying, which dropped to 82.9% in the third month. Though 100% effective one month after spraying, mortality due to deltamethrin spray dropped to 78.8% in the third month after spraying.

The involvement of HEWs in IRS as part of the community-based IRS strategy is indicated in the National Strategic Plan 2011-2015. This initiative receives funding support from the Global Fund. In FY 2012, FMOH requested PMI support to pilot the feasibility of integrating IRS into the existing HEP and decentralizing the organization of spray operations from the district to the community level in one district, with a focus on ensuring environmental compliance, quality of IRS operations, and building the local capacity. The pilot of community-based IRS was undertaken in 20 malarious *kebeles* of Kersa District, with the intention of testing the hypotheses that this model increases community participation and acceptance, reduces costs over the long term, and increases the sustainability of the program.

Under this model, mini-operational sites are established in each *kebele*. Health extension workers serve as IRS squad leaders and assume responsibility for managing store rooms, washers, and operators, and data collection and reporting. Spray operators are hired from the *kebeles* and do not require transport and camping facilities. Community-based IRS operations are closely supervised by the head of the District Health Office, the malaria focal person, and the environmental compliance officer, which each provide technical back-up when required.

Overall, the performance of the HEWs in organizing and conducting IRS operations in this pilot was found to be very positive, and quality assurance tests showed similar results to the district-based operations, indicating a high quality of spraying.

Based on this experience, PMI expanded this pilot to six districts during the spray round in 2013. PMI has been working to ensure that a comprehensive evaluation is carried out that addresses the quality of spraying, logistical management, proper storage, handling, and disposal of insecticides, and the financial costs of such an approach. Further expansion of this approach will depend on the outcome of this six district pilot. The Ethiopia PMI team will engage PMI headquarters in the review of the results of this pilot and in the decisionmaking about whether continuation and/or further expansion of this approach is warranted.

In the event that district councils of graduated districts fail to allocate funds and IRS operations are disrupted in high transmission risk areas, PMI will advocate that the FMOH and RHBs intervene. PMI will continue monitoring malaria case load data in those districts through routine HMIS and epidemic surveillance sentinel sites. If there is a need, PMI will provide required assistance to implement malaria control activities in those districts through focal spraying, LLIN distribution, RDTs and malaria treatment. PMI will continue entomological monitoring in the graduated districts to monitor entomological impact.

In 2013, PMI protected more than 1.5 million people living in the Oromia Regional State by spraying approximately 550,000 structures in the same 36 PMI-supported districts using carbamates (bendiocarb). PMI also assisted the spraying of up to 500,000 additional structures in the same 24 graduated districts by supporting microplanning, procurement of replacement equipment to fill gaps, and technical assistance as needed. In 2013, PMI undertook one spray round from August – October, just before the major malaria transmission season.

In addition to district-level implementation of IRS, PMI also provides support to the national and regional levels. At the national level, PMI participates in existing IRS working groups to support the FMOH in the development of guidelines, policies, and strategies, as well as providing operational support including provision of limited personal protective equipment. PMI also supports specific training in IRS operations as well as ensuring environmental compliance, insecticide safety, and performing entomological monitoring activities. At the regional (Oromia) level, PMI procures insecticides and equipment for IRS operations, supports annual IRS microplanning and training workshops, and provides operational funds for implementation and supervision. In addition to technical support, PMI provided a limited supply of personal protective equipment to the FMOH to strengthen environmental compliance efforts in areas outside of Oromia.

Entomologic Monitoring: In 2011, PMI's susceptibility tests, in addition to those undertaken by WHO, EHNRI and local universities showed high resistance to pyrethroids, resulting in the FMOH's decision to discontinue the use of pyrethroids for IRS beyond 2012. The FMOH now acknowledges that a long-term insecticide resistance strategy is crucial to ensure continued efficacy of IRS in Ethiopia. A national strategy for insecticide resistance management is currently under development, involving a range of stakeholders.

Building the capacity of district health offices to carry out key entomological monitoring activities as part of their annual malaria intervention plan is considered a crucial step in sustaining this effort. In collaboration with the FMOH and EHNRI, 26 districts representing different eco-epidemiological settings of the country were selected to serve as entomological surveillance sentinel sites in 2012. In October of last year, PMI collaborated with Addis Ababa University to train 24 malaria experts (from 24 districts) over the course of ten days on entomological monitoring and insecticide resistance testing. They further received intensive practical training that will enable them to perform the tests independently. By September of 2013, all 24 districts will complete insecticide resistance tests and submit a report based on their findings to PMI and the national Vector Control Working group.

PMI continued supporting entomological monitoring in 2012 in five sentinel sites (Table 5) and behavioral studies in three sites. Behavioral monitoring was conducted in IRS operation areas using deltamethrin and bendiocarb. In the deltamethrin-sprayed villages, the number of mosquitoes feeding on humans (by human landing catch method) dropped significantly after one month of spraying, but surged back to the pre-spray levels in the second and third months, while in the bendiocarb-sprayed village, biting was reduced significantly after spraying and remained low throughout the study period.

PMI is also monitoring the malaria vector population in areas affected by the GoE's new water and soil conservation program, where it is feared that the trenches created by this program will allow the vector to flourish.

Table 5. Insecticide Resistance Monitoring, 2012

Insecticide	Asendabo	Halaba	Zuway	Chewaka	Bahir dar
	Test Mortality %(number of mosquitoes tested)				
Permethrin	10.9 (110)	-	-	-	-
Propoxur	98.1(105)	99 (100)	100 (100)	96 (100)	100 (100)
Malathion	66.1 (115)	48 (100)	90 (100)	58(100)	26 (100)
Lambdacyhalothrin	25.7 (105)	-	-	-	-
Fenitrothion	99.1 (105)	100 (100)	99 (100)	100 (100)	100 (100)
Etofenoprox	8.7 (115)	-	-	-	23 (112)
DDT	3.8 (103)	0 (100)	13(100)	3 (100)	6 (100)
Bendiocarb	93.3 (105)	98 (100)	100 (100)	90 (100)	87 (100)
Deltamethrin	12.8 (115)	1(100)	27 (100)	12 (100)	44 (100)
Alphacypermethrin	24.8 (105)	-	-	-	50 (120)
Pirimiphos methyl	100 (105)	-	-	-	100 (100)

Challenges, Opportunities and Threats

As indicated in the national strategic plan, many challenges and limitations exist surrounding future Ethiopia IRS operations. Among them are: resistance to multiple insecticides by the primary malaria vector; epidemiological targeting of IRS to have the most impact; ensuring sustainability of the program; best use of limited portfolio of resources; re-plastering of houses after spraying resulting in decreased efficacy; and the need to improve pesticide management and environmental compliance. Given the high level of insecticide resistance, the spray program will have to shift to more expensive classes of insecticides, which will hinder the program's ability to sustain and/or scale up the program due to the limited funding available. Furthermore, it is not certain whether graduated districts are able to maintain IRS operations at previous coverage levels and quality.

Another major challenge is the presence of about 1,300 tons of obsolete insecticide (over 99% DDT), most of it pre-dating PMI, in more than 500 districts nationally that was managed by the FMOH and Regional Health Bureaus. Management and/or disposal of these obsolete pesticides will need a considerable level of financial and technical support. With USG interest in protecting environmental and human health in Ethiopia, PMI has supported an assessment to establish the inventory of obsolete insecticides at the district, zonal and regional levels in those districts where PMI currently or previously supported IRS. Different options for the obsolete insecticides' final disposal have been discussed with the FMOH, ORHB and other parties including the African Stockpile Program at the World Bank. In-country capacity to incinerate DDT using cement kilns was assessed in 2012 with inconclusive results. Currently PMI has offered technical assistance and logistical support to collect all the obsolete insecticides available in districts where PMI currently or previously supported IRS and transport it to a secure facility. We are awaiting approval of this plan by the FMOH.

Plans and Justification

PMI will maintain the FY 2013 level of IRS support by working closely with the FMOH, ORHB and other partners. With FY 2014 funding, approximately 550,000 structures will be sprayed with full support from PMI in 36 districts, protecting a population of approximately 1.5 million people. In addition, PMI will provide limited support for IRS operations in the 24 graduated districts. PMI will continue to focus on high malaria burden districts in Oromia and support environmental compliance activities, entomological monitoring in sentinel sites and insecticide resistance or susceptibility testing in selected sites.

Proposed activities with FY 2014 funding ($8,134,200)

FY 2014 PMI support for IRS operations in Oromia will be at the same level as in FY 2013, i.e., targeting about 550,000 structures for full support and providing minimal support in 24 graduated districts for IRS operations as described above. Based on feedback from graduated districts, evaluation of spray operations, discussions and priorities of ORHB to continue IRS implementation on their own and malaria case load, the graduation approach may be limited in its scale.

PMI's comprehensive support for IRS targeted districts in Oromia includes insecticide, operational funds, transportation, rehabilitation of district storage facilities, soak pits, personal protective equipment, environmental compliance, IEC and social mobilization, training on IRS techniques, and use and maintenance of spray pumps.

• **Procurement of insecticide ($4,500,000):** The exact allocations and specifications of insecticides will be adjusted upon completion and review of the 2013 IRS activities and the insecticide policy decision of FMOH.

• **Indoor residual spray operations ($3,000,000):** PMI will continue to support ORHB in planning, implementation and evaluation of IRS in Oromia. With FY 2014 funding, PMI will provide full support in 36 districts and minimal support in the 24 graduated districts. Based on the evaluation of 2013 operations, the number of structures to be sprayed may be adjusted.

• **Indoor residual spray training ($100,000):** PMI will support in-service training at federal and regional levels to increase the FMOH's and ORHB's capacity in planning and management of IRS operations, environmental compliance, and poison control.

• **Entomological capacity building and monitoring ($500,000):** Resistance monitoring will be carried out in 29 sites (24 sites using CDC bottle assays and five sites using WHO tube test) in different ecological zones of the country to continue documenting what is happening in the susceptibility/resistance status of the vector after change in the insecticide policy. Technical support will be provided to coordinate entomological monitoring activities implemented by the FMOH in sites outside of Oromia. Behavioral monitoring will be conducted to assess if vector behaviors change, especially early outdoor biting, in response to the changes in the insecticide used for IRS. Insecticide residual life monitoring to obtain evidence for the selection of best alternative insecticide also continues to be a priority activity.

• **Entomological supplies and equipment ($10,000):** Provide critical supplies, reagents and equipment for routine entomological monitoring activities and resistance and bionomic studies.

• **Entomological technical assistance ($24,200):** Provide two technical assistance visits from CDC/Atlanta for training, planning and monitoring entomological activities given the expansion of entomological surveillance up to the national level.

MALARIA IN PREGNANCY (MIP)

NMCP/PMI Objectives

Ethiopia has a relatively low ANC coverage rate compared to other countries in the region. The 2011 DHS indicated that for Ethiopia as a whole, only 34% of mothers received antenatal care from a heath professional for their most recent birth in the five years preceding the survey, although this demonstrated an improvement from the 28% noted in the 2005 DHS. One woman in every five (19%) made four or more ANC visits during the course of her pregnancy, up from 12% in 2005. The median duration of pregnancy at the time of the first antenatal visit is 5.2 months. Furthermore, although pregnant women are at greater risk of severe disease from malaria, overall they represent a small proportion of the total number of malaria patients in Ethiopia. In a study by Newman et al, a cross-sectional survey of placental parasitemia at a stable (relatively high) malaria transmission site in the sparsely populated Gambella Regional State noted 6.5% prevalence, whereas three other sites in unstable (i.e. low) transmission settings noted only 2.5% prevalence. Because of the relatively low prevalence of malaria infection during pregnancy, intermittent preventive treatment of pregnant women (IPTp) is not part of the Ethiopian National Malaria Prevention and Control Strategic Plan.

Guidelines from FMOH for malaria treatment including pregnancy are available at http://www.moh.gov.et/English/Resources/Documents/National%20malaria%20guidelines_2012 .pdf. Consistent with WHO guidance, these guidelines recommend oral quinine for uncomplicated *P. falciparum* malaria in the first trimester, and oral AL for the second and third trimesters. For uncomplicated mono-species *P. vivax* malaria, oral chloroquine is recommended in all trimesters. For severe malaria, pre-referral rectal artesunate and IV artesunate for inpatient treatment is recommended.

There is minimal if any ITN distribution via ANC clinics, except through one very small project that overlaps with PEPFAR. Distribution of ITNs via ANC is not part of the FMOH malaria control strategy. Approaches used by the FMOH to target pregnant women are to: (i) scale-up universal LLIN coverage and encourage households to have pregnant women use LLINs; and (ii) ensure availability of prompt diagnosis and treatment of clinical cases in pregnant women at health facilities. The LLIN replacement scheme proposed in the National Strategic Plans for Malaria Prevention and Control 2011-2015 is the policy framework for continuous LLIN distribution primarily through the HEP. Nearly all ITNs are distributed by HEWs through mass-campaigns every three years. Although the universal coverage strategy is to provide one ITN per 1.8 persons, the HEW is guided by a written instructions to make sure that pregnant mothers and children less than five years of age have preferential access to LLINs in these mass campaigns and educate communities to give priority to pregnant mothers and children, in case nets are not sufficient to cover whole family. Increasing ANC coverage is also one of the FMOH's priorities, and is supported by USAID/Ethiopia MNCH, family planning and reproductive health funding.

Progress During the Last 12 Months

The President's Malaria Initiative provided technical support to update the FMOH's malaria diagnosis and treatment guidelines that were published in early 2012. These contained recommendations regarding the use of anti-malarial drugs during pregnancy. These guidelines were reinforced through trainings of HEWs through iCCM roll out that discussed malaria prevention and case management in pregnancy. Social behavior change communication messages and training are being developed based on these guidelines.

Challenges, Opportunities and Threats

In Ethiopia, only 34% of women had received antenatal care from a skilled provider and only 10% were delivered by a skilled provider. The most important barrier to access to health services that women mentioned is availability of transport to a facility, followed by lack of money and distance to a health facility, according to the 2011 MIS. A major focus of ANC programs in Ethiopia is providing expanded access to quality healthcare through health centers and health posts, where PMI is supporting prompt access to diagnostic and treatment services for pregnant women. Furthermore, HEWs will play a key role in identifying and preferentially distributing LLINs to pregnant women in the communities.

Plans and Justification

President's Malaria Initiative continues to support the current FMOH policies that address pregnant women's special needs through malaria prevention and control, and improving prompt access to malaria diagnosis, and appropriate care and treatment services. Although IPTp itself is not part of the national strategic plan, with FY 2014 funding, PMI will support maternal and perinatal protection from malaria with Focused Antenatal Care (FANC) Services and Safe Motherhood and Adolescent Reproductive Health through an emphasis on anemia management and the prompt diagnosis and management of acute malaria in pregnant women. To implement these activities, PMI has leveraged the resources of other GHI activities, particularly those supported by PEPFAR and USAID/Ethiopia MNCH, family planning, and reproductive health funds, and will harmonize healthcare worker and midwifery training and education. This harmonization will focus on ensuring that health providers counsel mothers on early detection of anemia and illnesses with fever, the importance of iron and folate supplementation, as well as using a LLIN during pregnancy for the protection of the fetus. This activity will be closely coordinated with PMI support for case management strengthening and supportive supervision for healthcare workers at health centers and HEWs at health posts.

Proposed Activities with FY 2014 Funding ($300,000)

• **Expanding malaria in pregnancy services through safe motherhood and FANC ($300,000)**: PMI will leverage resources from TB and PEPFAR to strengthen MCH services. PMI will focus on pre-service education, especially on the three cadres identified as priority cadres by the GoE in the HSDP IV – midwives and nurse anesthetists – as well as pre-service education for HEWs. PMI will support pre-service training of HEWs and midwives to ensure that malaria will be focused in pre- and in-service training for management of acute malaria in pregnant women.

CASE MANAGEMENT

DIAGNOSIS

NMCP/PMI Objectives

In line with Ethiopia's long-standing policy that all patients with suspected malaria should receive a diagnostic test before treatment is prescribed, PMI has supported scale-up of quality assured diagnostic testing at both facility and community-level since its launch in Ethiopia. At health centers, PMI has supported procurement of microscopes, lab supplies, and reagents, and is scaling-up quality assurance systems for malaria microscopy and RDTs. At the community level, support is being provided for procurement of RDTs and training and supervision of HEWs in iCCM of the sick child, including performance of RDTs for managing acute febrile illnesses.

Progress During the Last 12 Months

An analysis by UNICEF of microplan data (figure below) indicates that Ethiopia has made significant progress in scaling-up diagnostic testing for malaria: the percentage of all malaria cases reported that were confirmed by RDT or microscopy increased from 67% in 2011 to 83% in 2012 (see Figure 5). Oromia has shown a significant achievement in reducing presumptive treatment of malaria from 99% in 2007 to 23% in 2013 (see Figure 6).

Figure 5: Proportion of malaria suspected cases tested with RDT or Microscopy in (a) 2010-2011 and (b) 2011-2012 (Microplan Data)

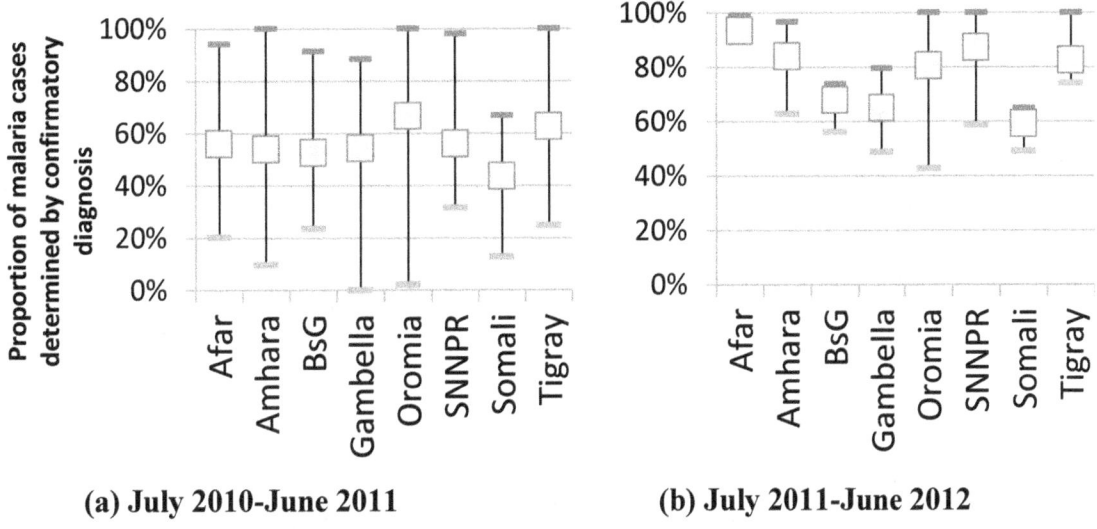

(a) July 2010-June 2011   (b) July 2011-June 2012

Figure 6: Percentage of clinically treated malaria cases out of total cases in Oromia Regional State from 2006/07-2011/12

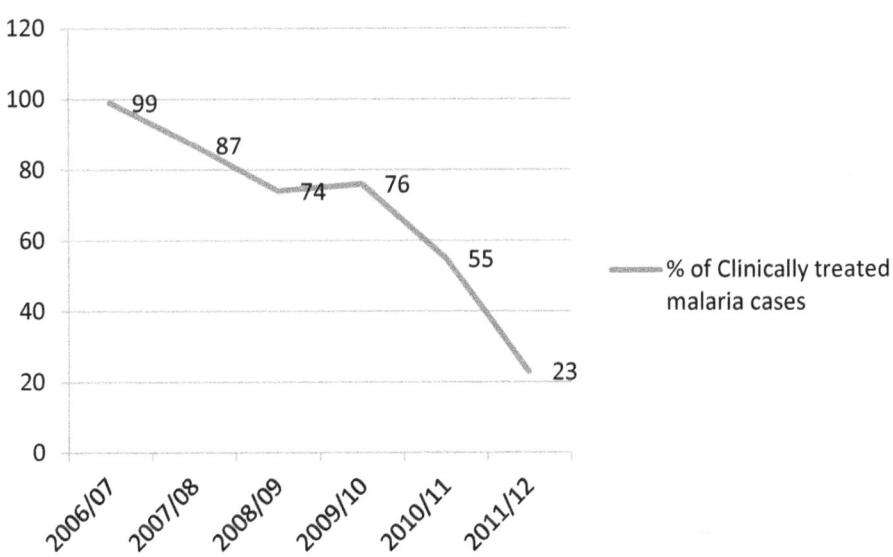

PMI procured and distributed 3.2 million RDTs to HEWs in Oromia and also filled gaps of RDTs in other parts of the country. In addition, 146 microscopes and microscopy kits for health centers and reference laboratories in eight regional states and two administrative cities were procured.

PMI-supported microscopy trainings are provided several times per year and are complemented by onsite supportive supervision and mentorship. PMI currently supports training and supervision of malaria diagnosis in 179 of the 700 health centers with laboratories in malarious areas in Oromia. PMI envisages scaling-up this support to all 700 facilities by 2015. Outside of Oromia Regional State, PMI also plans to provide enhanced facility-based supportive supervisions to 82, 31, and 61 health centers in Amhara, Tigray, and SNNPR regional states, respectively.

In order to reach more health facilities, PMI has built capacity of seven regional labs in five additional regional states to conduct cascade training and supervision of peripheral laboratories. PMI also leverages resources from PEPFAR to integrate malaria laboratory strengthening in 246 health facilities that are currently supported by PEPFAR programs and supportive supervision of HEWs in over 1500 health posts.

In addition, PMI has supported training of 506 laboratory personnel on integrated malaria-HIV laboratory diagnosis and quality assurance/quality control (QA/QC) system. Furthermore, 52 laboratory supervisors have received training of trainers training from regional reference labs in Oromia, Amhara, Tigray, Dire Dawa, and SNPPR. These supervisors are now planning to cascade basic trainings in all regional states of Ethiopia using funds from GoE and technical assistance from PMI.

Challenges, Opportunities and Threats

It has been recognized that there is insufficient human and financial resources to support blinded rechecking of blood slides for all health facilities at regional reference laboratories. Therefore, facilities that score greater than 95% on three successive rounds of rechecking will be considered "graduated" so that additional facilities can then undergo rechecking.

Progress has been made in expanding supportive supervision to more health facilities. Because of the very large number of health facilities in Ethiopia, only one-fifth of facilities in Oromia and a small number of facilities in other states are getting routine supervision for malaria diagnosis. PMI is exploring collaboration with PEPFAR to integrate supervision of malaria microscopy and RDTs into their supervision of laboratories in their focus areas. In addition, PMI will work to assist regional states to strengthen subregional reference laboratories and pilot the use of laboratory staff from graduated facilities to supervise nearby facilities that are not currently receiving supportive supervision.

Plans and Justification

PMI will build on the progress to-date in scaling-up diagnostic testing for malaria and accelerate expansion of quality assurance systems to cover more than 700 facilities in Oromia and other regional states. PMI will also expand training and support to all regional laboratories, to include Afar, Gambella, Harari, and Benishangul-Gumuz. PMI will further expand supervision to laboratories supported by PEPFAR, by integrating malaria supervision modules into their supervision tools and by training their supervisors in malaria microscopy and performance of RDTs.

President's Malaria Initiative will procure approximately 6 million RDTs, which will fully meet the requirements in Oromia and make a significant contribution to the requirements in the rest of the country, as projected using the forecast developed through a national level microplanning (*see Gap Analysis below*). Additional microscopes, lab supplies, and reagents also will be procured and distributed to laboratories in Oromia, Amhara, Tigray, and SNNPR.

There are about 3,000 health centers and 120 public hospitals that use microscopes. In the past, Global Fund and PEPFAR funding has been used to purchase some microscopes, but gaps remain. The exact numbers of facilities requiring microscopes is being refined and prioritized by FMOH, EHNRI, and RHBs. PMI also is building capacity to repair microscopes already in facilities. To promote standardization, PMI tries to ensure that malaria microscopes have similar formats and capabilities.

PMI will be building capacity for support supervision of malaria diagnosis in all facilities currently being supported by PEPFAR, which includes: 246 health facilities in Oromia, 12 in Somali, eight in Harari, and 12 in Dire Dawa. Building this capacity into existing supervision activities in these 278 additional facilities comes at minimal additional cost and will help move Ethiopia towards scaling up supervision activities to all facilities in the country.

President's Malaria Initiative will continue its support of clinical oversight of malaria diagnosis and case management activities of HEWs through an integrated supervision platform, and of clinicians at health centers through mentorship and supportive supervision. In addition, PMI will be supporting pre-service training of HEWs and clinicians in fever case management.

Table 6. RDT Gap Analysis, 2015

	2015
Total number of suspected malaria fever cases (confirmed plus clinical)	11,127,705
Country target for diagnostic coverage *(Baseline 83% in 2012 from UNICEF Microplan Data)*	100%
Diagnostic coverage by microscopy (%)	25%
Diagnostic coverage by RDT (%)	75%
Total number of RDTs needed (National) *(Microplanning data adjusted by a factor of 25% for epidemics)*	11,290,000
RDTs needed in Oromia	2,351,536
PMI contribution	6,000,000
Available RDT from GF and other sources	Not yet in place
Remaining Gap	5,290,000

Proposed Activities with FY 2014 Funding ($6,450,000)

• **Procurement of RDTs ($4,800,000):** PMI will procure and distribute 6 million multi-species RDTs mostly to health posts. This will meet the projected needs of the country.

• **Support for quality assurance system for microscopy and RDTs ($900,000):** Technical and programmatic support to health facility laboratories will be scaled up to more than 700 facilities in Oromia and other regional states. Additionally operational support will be provided to all regional reference laboratories in Ethiopia as well as major regional hospitals. This will include support for refresher training, supervision, other QA/QC activities, and program monitoring. Training and accreditation will be provided to laboratory supervisors.

• **Procurement of lab equipment/supplies ($750,000):** PMI will support further procurement of approximately 220 microscopes and 700 laboratory kits to provide essential supplies and reagents to laboratories that conduct malaria microscopy.

• **Provide supportive supervision to HEWs (see Treatment section):** Continued support will be provided for integrated supervision of HEWs, which will include observation of management of patients.

TREATMENT

NMCP/PMI Objectives

One of the goals of the National Strategic Plan for malaria 2011-2015 is to treat all confirmed malaria cases with appropriate antimalarial drugs and manage all severe cases according to the new treatment guideline. Current treatment policy recommends AL and chloroquine as the first-line drug for the treatment of uncomplicated *P. falciparum* malaria and *P. vivax* malaria, respectively. For infants <5 kg of body weight and pregnant women in the first trimester, quinine should be administered. Rectal artesunate has been adopted as pre-referral treatment for severe malaria at the health post level. Intravenous/intramuscular artesunate (or IV/IM quinine, if artesunate is not available) is recommended for treatment of severe cases at the health centers and hospitals.

Progress During Last 12 Months

To date, PMI has procured 9.35 million AL treatment doses for Oromia. As part of the national support, PMI has also procured 7.88 million doses of chloroquine, 56,458 quinine doses, and 108,000 doses of rectal and 86,000 IV/IM artesunate. In addition, PMI has also supported the microplanning of malaria commodities at the district level. This exercise has significant importance in allocation and distribution of malaria commodities based on malaria morbidity at the district level. Based on this microplanning, ACT needs have decreased by 1.5 million doses, as a result of improved planning, decreasing malaria burden, and increased utilization of diagnostic testing (see Figure 7).

The President's Malaria Initiative is working with ORHB, FMOH, and other implementing partners to support health worker training at both the health center and health post levels, including the roll-out of iCCM to community-level health posts in 301 districts in 6 regional states. In addition, 194 clinical staff have been trained on appropriate fever case management. PMI will also support activities to improve performance standards and quality of the pre-service and in-service training; and support in-service training programs for clinical officers and HEWs through the Integrated Refresher Training Program, implemented by the FMOH.

The President's Malaria Initiative is supporting District Health Office staff in monitoring and supervision of health centers, and supports health center staff in their monitoring and supervision of health posts. During the past year, 280 health centers and 1,539 health posts were supervised in 301 *woredas*. This supervision is being integrated into established, USAID/Ethiopia-supported family planning/reproductive health and MNCH activities. The supervision is ensuring that case management is implemented effectively and in-line with FMOH guidelines. PMI, along with other partners, is assisting in reviewing the quality and competency of the supervisors, and help to support refresher trainings and coaching, to further improve supervisors' capacity. This includes providing training materials and checklists as well as transportation and other costs to ensure the supervision is actually taking place.

In 2010, PMI supported a quantitative study to document the extent and nature of adherence to malaria treatment (AL). Overall adherence was low in the population evaluated, with only 55% of patients adhering to their full treatment course. This study also showed a significantly lower adherence (37%) in children compared to adults. It recommended enhancing training and supervision for all health workers to provide full instructions on malaria medications and to support and utilize HEWs in the management of malaria medications and promoting adherence, which will also help guide SBCC approaches.

Figure 7. Malaria Treatment Commodities Requirement Trends (per Microplan data) for 2011–12 and 2012–13)

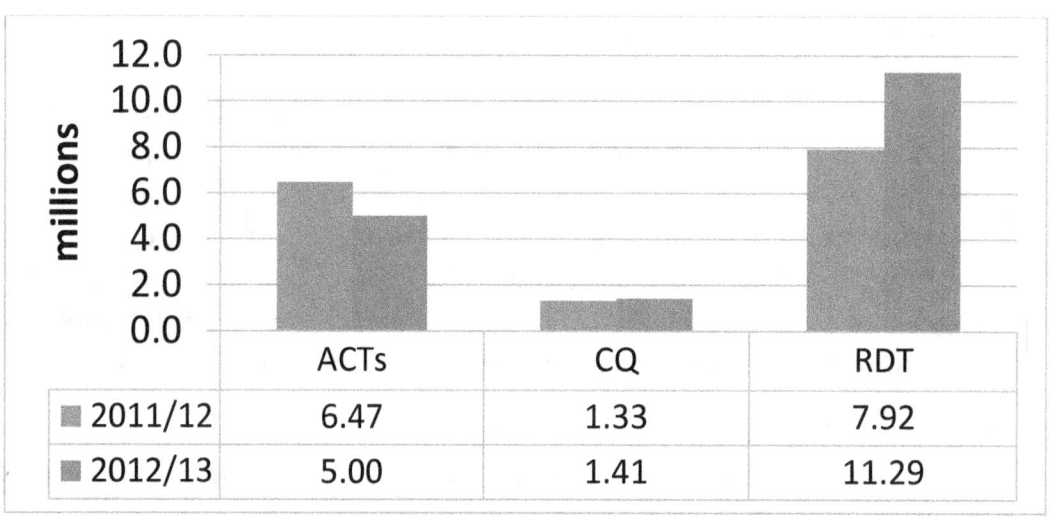

	ACTs	CQ	RDT
▪ 2011/12	6.47	1.33	7.92
▪ 2012/13	5.00	1.41	11.29

Opportunities, Challenges and Threats

Ethiopia revised the malaria treatment guidelines in 2012. Major challenges in malaria treatment include clinicians' adherence to treatment guidelines, patients' adherence to treatment, and maintaining a continuous supply of effective medicines at the health post level and private facilities. In 2011, a baseline assessment conducted in 122 health centers in Dire Dawa and Oromia regional states revealed that 51% of clinicians tend to treat patients with ACT even though blood film test results were negative, and only 15% of clinicians reported to give priority for assessing other causes of acute febrile illness in the absence of positive malaria microscopy diagnosis. Although there are enough ACTs imported into the county, there are uneven distributions to health facilities and there is an imperfect and poorly developed system for redistributing medicines between districts. Furthermore, ensuring adherence to malaria treatment has been challenging, especially in children.

Plans and Justification

Due to uncertainties related to future funding availability from the Global Fund and other donors, the gap in ACT requirements may increase from 2012 onwards. With FY 2014 funding, PMI is procuring 3.8 million AL treatments for Oromia and to fill gaps in other parts of Ethiopia (Table 7). PMI will also procure chloroquine, quinine, and rectal andIV artesunate as part of its national support (Table 8).

The FMOH has little interaction with the private sector in malaria care and treatment with the exception of a small USAID-funded project called Private Public Partnerships, which involves data and resource sharing with private health facilities. While there are few avenues available for PMI to cooperate with or understand the private sector via the FMOH, this project will be a starting point for PMI to understand some of the malaria-related issues and might someday encourage the FMOH to adopt more activities involving private sector cooperation.

Table 7. ACT Gap Analysis, 2015

	2015
Total number of suspected malaria fever cases	11,127,705
Country target for diagnostic and treatment coverage	100%
Total confirmed cases of *P. falciparum* (67.8%) plus clinically treated cases (FY2011 microplan)	4,347,903
Number of ACT treatment doses needed (National) *(Microplanning data adjusted for epidemics)*	**5,000,000**
Number of treatment doses needed (Oromia)	**1,044,295**
ACT available from PMI resource	**3,800,000**
ACT available from GF and other sources	**Not yet known**
Remaining Gap	**1,200,000**

Table 8. Gap Analysis for Chloroquine, 2015

	2015
Total number of suspected malaria fever cases *(Microplanning data adjusted by a factor of 30% for epidemics, under-reporting of negative cases and contingency)*	11,127,705
Country target for diagnostic coverage (Baseline 83% in 2012 from Microplan Data)	100%
Total *P. vivax* (32.2%)	1,174,559
Number of chloroquine treatments doses needed (National)	**1,140,000**
Number of chloroquine treatments doses needed (Oromia)	277,638
Chloroquine available from PMI	**1,500,000**
Chloroquine available from GF and other sources	0
Remaining gap	0

Proposed Activities with FY 2014 Funding ($6,750,000)

• **Procurement of ACTs for *P. falciparum*, chloroquine, and primaquine for *P. vivax*, pre-referral treatments and drugs for severe malaria ($5,500,000):** PMI will support the procurement and distribution of 3.8 million AL treatments to meet the needs for Oromia based on the district-level microplan as well as a contingency amount for national-level distribution by the FMOH to fill gaps in other parts of the country. PMI will support the procurement and distribution of the entire estimated national need for chloroquine (i.e., 1.5 million treatments) and other antimalarial drugs, including drugs for severe disease and pre-referral care (i.e., rectal and parenteral artesunate) and primaquine. Chloroquine, pre-referral treatment, and drugs for severe malaria will be tested for quality at accredited laboratories following standardized protocol prior to shipment to Ethiopia.

• **Support for supervision and monitoring of HEWs in providing malaria treatment ($600,000):** Support to supervision and monitoring of malaria treatment at health centers and health posts in eastern Oromia, eastern Amhara, and Dire Dawa and Harari regional states (which represent one third of all of the HEWs in the country) will be continued. Several activities are included in this on-site supervision ensuring that HEWs: (i) have enough RDTs and other supplies necessary to use RDTs at community-level; (ii) use RDTs correctly; (iii) adhere to national malaria case management guidelines, and provide the correct treatment to RDT-confirmed cases; (iv) correctly dispose of RDTs; and (v) correctly report number of suspected fever cases tested, diagnosed, and treated. About 300 district health offices, 770 health centers and more than 1,500 health posts will receive this supportive supervision. More than 300 health workers, including HEWs, will receive in-service training in reviewing new malaria case management guidelines, on-site supervision, and ensuring that case management reporting is complete and accurate.

• **Private sector support to case management ($100,000):** PMI will work with the regional health bureaus and 83 private health facilities in four regional states, including Oromia Regional State, to increase access to quality malaria services, including diagnostic testing and free antimalarial treatment to the clients.

• **Support for expansion of iCCM activities in Western Oromia Regional State ($550,000):** PMI and other partners also have supported training on iCCM, RDT use, and rectal artesunate to all HEWs in Ethiopia including Oromia (with PMI supporting about one third of the 27,000 HEWs, 200 health officers, and 2,000 nurses), with the exception of three zones in Western Oromia Regional State. There are approximately 3,000 HEWs in the remaining three zones in Oromia that still require this training. In order to cover all zones in Oromia, additional support for iCCM activities including training and ongoing supervision, will be provided to these three remaining zones.

• **Pre-service training of HEWs and clinicians in fever case management (no additional funding required):** PMI will support pre-service training of HEWs and midwives for integrated malaria case management. PMI will also ensure that malaria-specific updates for technical materials and guidelines are provided to USG supported midwifery training and capacity building programs, including PEPFAR-funded activities focusing on the prevention of mother-to-child-transmission of HIV (PMTCT). In addition capacity of 31 universities will be strengthened to provide quality training of ambulatory patient management. On site mentoring will be provided for clinicians, nurses and doctors in 100 selected health centers to improve malaria case management.

PHARMACEUTICAL MANAGEMENT

NMCP/PMI Objectives

The FMOH and PMI have been working to address multiple supply chain problems within all layers of the national drug management system, including malaria commodity bottlenecks, stockouts, and expiry. In 2005, the FMOH developed a Pharmaceutical Logistics Management Plan (PLMP) and later created the PFSA. Through mostly PEPFAR and Global Fund support, the FMOH radically redesigned the governance, policies, and infrastructure of the existing logistics system, establishing drug distribution "hubs" to directly supply health centers, health posts, and hospitals. Because of its complexity and cost, the new pharmacy supply chain system was slowly implemented and essential malaria commodities are still being largely distributed through other parallel donor-supported systems. Up until 2012, PMI has imported and distributed most of its malaria commodities (including ACTs) for Oromia Regional State through UNICEF per FMOH guidance, to be consistent with and complementary to Global Fund processes.

With PMI support, UNICEF has also conducted annual malaria commodity microplanning activities to gather district-level data about malaria commodity inventories and estimated future malaria commodity requirements along with malaria morbidity reports. PMI also has supported strengthening of PFSA. As the capacities within PFSA improve and as PFSA takes over more and more responsibilities for pharmacy supply chains in Ethiopia, PMI will transition to distributing its commodities through this system. The Ethiopian FMHACA, a recently reorganized agency of FMOH, needs strengthening on many levels. It is responsible for regulating and registering medicines and ensuring the safety and quality monitoring of all medicines. It is also responsible for establishing and implementing quality assurance systems for the country, including post-marketing drug quality monitoring. PMI strengthens drug quality and safety monitoring capacities at FMHACA via post-marketing surveillance activities including use of minilabs. The minilabs are used to collect drug samples and provide preliminary field testing at the customs check points, at the airports, and border ports of entry. The long term vision of PMI is for continued post-marketing surveillance and strengthening of FMHACA's regional laboratories capacity to provide confirmatory testing and expanding this to regional branch laboratories

Progress During the Last 12 Months

The President's Malaria Initiative supported PFSA by embedding qualified personnel within their facilities, and providing resources for the development of standard operating procedures and forms for the quantification, requisition, drug exchange/transfer and management of malaria commodities. A new medication record form was also designed. In addition, PMI has improved malaria commodity management in a number of public health facilities, including 212 in Oromia and 77 in other Regional States. These included 39 health posts, 19 hospitals and 200 health centers through improved training and supportive supervision. Malaria drug management data is now reported bi-monthly for all these facilities, including data on availability and expiry of antimalarial drugs, staff availability and capacity, and accurate reporting of antimalarial drug consumption. The data allows for monitoring and tracking of PMI- and FMOH-supported distribution of malaria commodities to health facilities.

In support of the FMHACA, PMI conducted a rapid assessment of Ethiopia's pharmaceutical quality assurance system and established a post-marketing drug quality monitoring program in five locations in Oromia, including the establishment of drug testing mini-labs and the training of GoE staff on drug sampling and testing. The third round of drug sampling was completed and the laboratory confirmatory testing of the second round is ongoing. To date, the results of this monitoring program indicate that the number of antimalarial drugs available in the public and private sectors in Ethiopia is limited, with most drugs sampled passing the drug quality control testing. In 2013, PMI expanded the post-market drug quality monitoring program beyond Oromia (including establishing additional sentinel locations at the boarders in Afar, Amhara, Somali, Gambella, and SNNPR) and further improved the regulatory capabilities of the FMHACA. PMI also ensured that the activities are coordinated with other USG implementing partners and in-country stakeholders in a context of a changing PLMP and the nascent establishment of the PFSA.

With PMI support, UNICEF facilitated microplanning meetings with participants from all malaria-affected *woredas* and zones in Oromia annually since 2009, and in all regional states since 2011 to determine the requirements of ACTs and RDTs at the district level. The microplan is continuously being updated when distributions of commodities to the zones and districts occur. The updated microplan is being shared with PMI implementing partners to inform them when commodities will and should be available in the locations of implementation (e.g., health facilities). Partners then report back to PMI on commodity availability.

The ACT and RDT requirements were determined based on consumption records from previous years at health facilities and health posts level of each *woreda*. The microplan considered the numbers of newly constructed health facilities and those expected to be operational in the following year. The results have subsequently been used to estimate the needs of pediatric and adult tablets of chloroquine to treat *P. vivax* malaria, and to prioritize and rationalize malaria commodity distributions through the year, based upon updated available inventory of supplies and epidemiological reports of increased local malaria activity (such as "hot-spot" districts). With FY 2014 funding, PMI will continue to support FMOH and all regional states in Ethiopia in this microplanning process for malaria commodities that is now recognized as a best practice.

Challenges, Opportunities and Threats

Previous PMI-funded pharmaceutical facility baseline assessment surveys and ongoing reports reveal continued supply chain problems for malaria drugs in all regional states. There continue to be focal shortages and stockouts of ACTs (especially pediatric doses) and chloroquine; expired drugs; weak inventory control tools; inadequate medication records; and poorly organized and inadequate storage facilities.

The large geographical areas with many remote regions and seasonal rains cause major challenges to maintaining malaria commodity supply chains. The emerging capacities of PFSA and FMHACA provide an opportunity to take on more responsibility for pharmacy supply chains and antimalarial drug quality monitoring in the future. Improving availability of malaria diagnostics from RDTs and microscopy promises to reduce ACT requirements. Threats include uncertainty in resources from the Global Fund which could impede progress in malaria control.

Plans and Justification

Strengthening pharmaceutical and malaria commodity supply chains will be a long term PMI requirement. The microplanning process has been recognized as a best practice in Ethiopia to the extent that it was expanded beyond Oromia Regional State to include all of Ethiopia. Strengthening antimalarial drug management will also be needed throughout Ethiopia through a closer working relationship with PFSA. There will be an ongoing need to ensure quality of antimalarial drugs in Ethiopia to support quality malaria care and treatment in partnership with FMHACA.

Proposed Activities with FY 2014 Funding ($1,400,000)

• **Strengthening of Antimalarial Drug Management ($750,000):** PMI will help sustain and expand the malaria drug management program from the current approximately 200 health centers covering approximately two-thirds of the malaria risk areas within Oromia, to support for strengthening health systems and pharmacy logistics for the PFSA in all regional states of Ethiopia. The program will continue to focus on:

- Improving the management of malaria commodities, including quantification, requisition, drug exchange/transfer, and expiry tracking/disposal;
- Improving the storage, organization, and security of drugs within health facilities and zonal/districts;
- Promoting the rational use of malaria drugs by training of PFSA and health facility level staff in drug management, as well as through on-site supervision; and
- Implementing the PMI end-use verification program, ensuring that antimalarial drugs distributed through PMI funding support are available at facilities and reach beneficiaries.

• **Strengthening PFSA pharmaceutical management capacities ($250,000):** PMI will provide direct support to PFSA to improve management of malaria commodities, including quantification, requisition, drug exchange/transfer, and expiry tracking/disposal in other regional states. In addition PFSA capacity will be built to procure, prepare and distribute quality reagents such as Giemsa solution for malaria diagnosis.

• **Strengthening of drug quality monitoring ($400,000):** PMI will continue to sustain and further improve the Ethiopia FMHACA's drug quality assurance program by:

- Support post-marketing drug quality monitoring in six sentinel sites in all regional states
- Training staff of FMHACA central and five regional laboratories on quality control tests of antimalarials
- Strengthening the GoE's central and regional quality control laboratories through training, technical assistance, sample collection, supportive supervision, and supply of equipment and reagents to FMHACA laboratories.
- Improving data use and subsequent policy and regulatory measures.

• **Microplanning surveys for estimating annual requirements and for assisting with distributions of malaria commodities:** (*see M&E section*) With FY 2014 funding, PMI will continue to support FMOH through microplanning meetings with participants from all malaria-affected *woredas* and zones in Ethiopia to determine the requirements of ACT treatments and RDTs at the district level. PMI-supported microplan activities will be increasingly integrated with and harmonized with PFSA and FMOH's *woreda*-based planning activities in the future.

MONITORING AND EVALUATION

NMCP/PMI Objectives

Epidemic Detection and Response

Malaria epidemics in Ethiopia have been documented since the 1930s. A catastrophic malaria epidemic in 1958 was responsible for an estimated 3 million clinical cases of malaria and 150,000 deaths. Since 1958, major epidemic years have occurred approximately every five to eight years (Tulu, A. N. "Malaria", In: Kloos, H. and Zein, A. Z., The Ecology of Health and Disease in Ethiopia, 1993, West View Press Boulder, San Francisco, Oxford, pp. 341-352). Guidelines for Malaria Epidemic Prevention and Control were updated in 2012 with support of PMI and are available on the FMOH's website. These new guidelines detail the human vulnerability factors, including population movement, as well as meteorological factors, such as rainfall, temperature, and humidity, that affect the occurrence of epidemics. The revised guidelines include setting detection thresholds at the health post level and strategies for mapping malaria micro-foci or micro-clusters.

Current methods for epidemic detection in Ethiopia rely on passive case detection of clinically diagnosed cases at health posts and health centers. In this system, the median weekly clinically diagnosed malaria cases over the previous five years are charted. Thresholds are set by either the third quartile (second highest number from the five previous year's data for that week) or the previous year's number of cases in that week multiplied by two. If the number of cases in a given week exceeds the set threshold, the health worker is to report a potential epidemic. A rapid assessment team is then dispatched to confirm that an epidemic exists or is threatening, establish the cause and scale of the epidemic, and identify local capacity to deal with it. The guidelines recommend presumptive mass fever treatment with ACTs for fever cases if the test positivity rate is ≥50%. A stock of 20% of ACTs is to be held at the regional level for epidemic response. If there is potential for continued transmission, IRS will be implemented. For this reason, all districts with a potential for epidemics are advised to reserve a stock of insecticide for epidemic response and spraying operations would begin following either a three- or six-day training period for local spray operators.

In 2009, a Public Health Emergency Management (PHEM) surveillance system was developed to cover the entire country encompassing reporting from health posts, health centers, and hospitals. The PHEM aims to be a weekly multi-disease reporting system that collects a range of malaria indicators that are mostly related to outpatient malaria morbidity. The PHEM surveillance reporting covered 80% of malarious districts throughout Ethiopia as of 2012, aiming to provide weekly reports from all health facilities, including health posts, through district health offices. Functionally, though, most districts only provide monthly reports, and health post reporting has lagged behind. The PHEM depends on accurate and timely information being reported from HEWs and health facilities, so building that capacity though the health post level is essential. Malaria cases are reported by two age groups (less than five and more than five years of age) including clinical malaria (outpatient and inpatient), confirmed malaria by species, malaria in pregnancy, and severe malaria/anemia in those less than five years of age. Although coverage is rapidly improving, this system is not yet fully operational at regional and national scale. Assuming that improved IRS coverage and LLIN use will reduce malaria transmission, the focus of malaria control and elimination will turn toward enhancing surveillance with the aim of halting ongoing transmission.

There are 143 "hotspot" districts with the highest reported number of cases as identified by PHEM. Only three of the ten epidemic detection sites currently supported by PMI are located in hotspot districts. The ten epidemic detection sites that PMI support are sub-district primary health unit catchment areas, with a total population of 450,000; they have enhanced surveillance and lab capacity, with weekly SMS reporting from the health post level. Both the hotspots and the ten epidemic detection sites are part of PHEM. The only differences are the extra surveillance enhancements at the ten sub-district sites, with real-time reporting capability from all included health posts and with continuous PMI data access via website and compiled monthly reports. PMI is in discussion with EHNRI/PHEM to scale up SMS or similar electronic weekly reporting from other health posts to improve timeliness of reporting in all PHEM sites, beyond the initial ten epidemic detection sites in Oromia.

The data gathered at these ten epidemic detection sites were essential input into the ongoing PMI impact evaluation, and such data will likely be important in subsequent periodic impact evaluations. The experiences developed at these sites have informed the FMOH as it has expanded the PHEM. It is anticipated that over the next few years, as the PHEM is fully scaled-up and is reliably providing complete and timely data, that these epidemic detection sites will be phased out and fully incorporated into PHEM with transferred capacity.

Monitoring & Evaluation

With PMI support, a National Malaria M&E Plan was recently developed. This plan aims to coordinate the collection, analysis, and management of malaria data to inform programmatic decisions and to assess whether the goals of the National Strategic Plan for Malaria Prevention and Control 2011 – 2015 (*see Strategy section*) are being achieved.

Currently, Ethiopia has a paper-based system of data collection at the health facility level; however, these data have not always been optimally analyzed or used for decision-making and resource allocation at the local, regional, or national level. Consequently, Ethiopia's FMOH is in the process of revising the HMIS. This revised HMIS, which includes a total of 106 indicators and is primarily supported via funds from PEPFAR and the Global Alliance for Vaccines and Immunization, aims to provide one standardized set of health indicators nationally. Unfortunately, HMIS reports are quarterly reporting from health centers and hospitals at district level (but no data reporting from health post) and reports of these data are not published for one or two years after they are collected. The most relevant and accurate data contained in these reports are inpatient cases and malaria deaths, although outpatient reporting is now over 50%. There are only two malaria-specific indicators in the HMIS:

- Malaria cases reported per 1,000 population, disaggregated into clinical and confirmed cases, with the latter further disaggregated by species, i.e., *P. falciparum*/other, among:
    - children <5 years of age, and
    - people at least five years of age; and

- Malaria case fatality rate among:
    - children <5 years of age [in-patients]
    - people at least 5 years of age [in-patients]

PMI supports the PHEM system, which aims for weekly malaria morbidity reports from hospitals, health centers and rural health posts. PMI's support is targeted to enhance reporting from rural health posts where half of all malaria morbidity is detected and treated, and to enable reporting of more complete RBM-MERG indicators on a weekly basis.

Progress During the Last 12 Months

The malaria module was removed from the Ethiopia DHS 2011 and an MIS survey was conducted in the same year separately due to a variety of technical and practical reasons. In particular, because of the focal nature of malaria in Ethiopia related to altitude strata, the sampling frame for a malaria survey is quite different from that of a general health survey. The sampling frame for the MIS focuses solely on areas with malaria risk (i.e., <2500 meters elevation). In addition, because of the highly seasonal nature of malaria transmission in Ethiopia, it has not been optimal to include malaria into the DHS, which have been conducted in the dry season. Therefore, PMI support will only be provided for MIS.

The current operational research activity on assessing the utility of conducting serologic assessment for malaria-specific antibodies will soon be underway and could provide information to guide PMI on the utility of collection of biomarkers in household surveys in settings where malaria transmission is very low.

Epidemic Detection and Response

President's Malaria Initiative is providing support for the development of a strengthened Epidemic Surveillance and Response (ESR) system in Oromia at the community, district, zonal, and regional levels. In order to detect epidemics quickly, PMI has started supporting strengthening of the alert system and health worker trainings for early epidemic detection.

In line with the GoE's desire to develop a high-quality, broadly-based malaria detection, investigation and response system, PMI supported the development of a strengthened ESR system at selected surveillance sites in Oromia. Health facilities were purposefully selected based on the epidemiological profile of the catchment area and health facility personnel were trained in data collection and reporting malaria indicators beyond the limited indicators collected in the HMIS. Designated health facility personnel were trained in data collection and reporting. Data collection began in February 2010 at ten epidemic detection sites in Oromia Regional State centered around health centers and their satellite health posts. PMI is now collecting data from ten districts with an entire population base of about 400,000 people, simultaneously observing malaria morbidity from health posts and health centers. This approach has promptly detected nearly all important malaria events within these catchment areas, improving the context and information derived from the surveillance data over time.

The objective of this intervention is to understand how increases of malaria cases and epidemic outbreaks occur at the community and sub-community level, as well as piloting approaches to documenting this process prospectively (e.g., by exploring whether travel history outside of the local village is related to malaria risk). Work at the epidemic detection sites also is providing operational data, which will allow PMI to understand how health centers become gradually affected by increases in case numbers or epidemic outbreaks at community and sub-community level, including with regards to patient access and flow, use of commodities, and work load of health facility staff.

The ESR data has confirmed the overall low incidence of severe malaria that is currently observed at facilities throughout Ethiopia. Since 2010 it detected four small malaria outbreaks, including a relapsing fever outbreak. The roll-out of SMS reporting at health post level to provide more robust, real-time data reporting has included all ten sites. In the first 33 months of surveillance at these ten sites, five small epidemics were detected among a total population for 430,000 people, with 256,095 total outpatients, 112,734 persons were tested for malaria, 28,450 having confirmed malaria diagnosis (*P. falciparum* (54%), *P. vivax* (46%), with 99 malaria inpatient admissions, and two malaria deaths).

In addition to these activities, PMI is supporting a study to assess whether schools could be a platform for detecting epidemics. School absenteeism, along with other easily collected information, will be compared to information collected at the health facility and community level to determine whether they may serve as an early warning indicator of an epidemic in the surrounding community. Information from a PMI-supported study of facility based malaria reporting in Oromia Regional State is being included in the soon to be completed malaria impact evaluation report.

Monitoring & Evaluation

Malaria risk maps: Given the varying epidemiologic profile of Ethiopia, resource allocation for malaria prevention and control activities must be targeted strategically. Malaria risk mapping is critical to improve targeting PMI and other program resources, and to track progress at the community level. PMI supported the development of a detailed malaria risk map in Oromia, identifying areas at risk for malaria, including epidemic-prone areas, based on data available from cross-sectional school-based surveys. Due to the low malaria prevalence only a crude risk map could be developed so far. It is expected that further analysis of samples using serology as well as analysis of prospective health facility data will ensure the development of a risk map with greater resolution. Of note, EHNRI has established serology testing capacity at the national level. They are currently testing the samples collected from a school-based survey. Preliminary results show that microscopy prevalence ranged from 0-12%, but serologic prevalence provided more variability from 0-60%. Several sites with 0% microscopy prevalence had higher serologic prevalence and furthermore, sites with serology prevalence of 0% provide invaluable information about longer malaria exposure.

Results are expected to be available from these studies by late 2013. In addition, WHO has been developing a nationwide risk map based on incidence and climate data. These efforts will be coordinated with the Oromia-specific data contributing to the development of the national map.

Malaria Indicator Survey (MIS): PMI supported the 2011 MIS, which assessed coverage, access, and use of malaria interventions. The final report is currently available on the FMOH website (*see Indicators section*). PMI not only financially supported this activity, but also provided significant technical assistance in all areas including all data collection and analytic support. The results showed a continued low prevalence of malaria by microscopy at 1.3% below 2,000 meters, with very low (0.1%) prevalence above 2,000 meters altitude.

A DHS was completed in early 2011 with results released in early 2012. This survey, though, did not include a malaria module.

Malaria Impact Evaluation: PMI is supporting an impact evaluation to determine impact of malaria control interventions since 2000 on malaria mortality and morbidity in Ethiopia. This analysis will consider all available data and contributions from all donors and the FMOH. A final comprehensive report from this impact evaluation is expected in late 2013, and a RBM Progress and Impact Series report will be published in 2014.

Malaria commodities microplans: PMI supported annual microplanning meetings with participants from all malaria-affected *woredas* and zones in Oromia since 2009 and for all of Ethiopia since 2011 to determine the requirements of RDTs, ACTs, and LLINs at district level. This exercise also provides annual reports of malaria case data from district health officials. The main purpose of these microplans is to develop a "bottom-up" needs-based plan, where malaria commodity requirements are identified by staff at the district level based on practical needs backed up by credible malaria morbidity and malaria commodity consumption, expiry, and inventory reports, rather than the usual "top down" push system, where distributions are estimated at the federal level. Besides quantification, microplanning is also used for prioritizing distribution of commodities and for monitoring consumption. In addition to the commodity quantification, microplanning also gathers district level data on malaria cases on an annual basis, which serves as an audit to assess completeness of malaria reporting of the routine surveillance system. This triangulation has been very useful in the PMI impact evaluation and other details are mentioned in the MOP background and epidemic sections. The microplan is being updated annually when commodities are distributed to the zones and districts. As mentioned elsewhere, it is expected that the microplanning process will be increasingly integrated and harmonized with PFSA and with FMOH's *woreda*-based planning processes in the future.

Field Epidemiology and Laboratory Training Program: Ethiopia began its FELTP in October 2008 with technical assistance from CDC as a two year, full-time, postgraduate competency-based training program consisting of about 25% class work and 75% field residency. Trainees are closely supervised and provide epidemiologic service to the FMOH. Graduates of FELTP will receive a Master's Degree in Public Health and Field Epidemiology. The program will join the African Field Epidemiology Network and work through the Ethiopian Public Health Association and EHNRI. In 2011, three Ethiopian FELTP residents supported a comprehensive evaluation of PMI's ten epidemic detection sites. In late 2012, three FELTP residents participated (along with a CDC Epidemic Intelligence Officer) in a *P. vivax* therapeutic efficacy trial with chloroquine versus AL with or without primaquine after G6PD testing. Another FELTP resident has nearly completed a project that investigates the feasibility of using dried tube specimens of standard concentrations of previously laboratory cultured *P. falciparum* as a reagent to assess the quality of malaria RDTs and the performance of health care workers in performing RDTs in field conditions (an abstract authored by the FELTP resident will be presented at the ASTMH 2013 meeting). Another FELTP resident is finalizing a protocol to investigate the epidemiology of reported malaria illness in Addis Ababa, and to determine travel histories, verify laboratory evidence, etc. in order to determine whether there are local foci of malaria transmission within Addis Ababa city limits.

Challenges, Opportunities and Threats

Microplans, while a very valuable annual activity, do not provide perfect estimates of resource and commodity requirements. Ultimately, in an epidemic-prone setting such as Ethiopia, redistribution of resources among or between districts may be needed to meet local needs that could not have been accurately forecasted from available data; such flexible redistribution plans or processes are typically not available. The PFSA does not yet have the capacity to meet the dynamic demands of the malaria transmission season or to respond promptly to urgent malaria medication stockouts. Some malaria commodities cost substantially less when ordered six or more months in advance, and some commodities have expiry dates of only two years; these factors create additional costs and increased risk of waste when logistics systems have slow procurement and customs clearance processes, slow, infrequent, and inflexible delivery cycles, and an inability to redistribute resources in the periphery based upon current malaria caseloads that fluctuate locally from year to year and season to season.

In addition, many districts have inadequate epidemic preparedness plans and lack sufficient contingency funds to respond. Lack of skilled health personnel and poor coordination and management compounds the problem. Although District Health Offices and Zonal Health Bureaus are instructed by national guidelines to have a 10-15% stockpile of malaria commodities, this is often not feasible due to planning and funding restrictions or increased clinical demand for these supplies. The ability to detect and respond to epidemics is also restricted by the existing HMIS, which is based upon reporting from only health centers and hospitals on a quarterly basis. While the PHEM system that aims for weekly malaria reporting is rapidly improving, this system has not yet been linked to a process that can redistribute malaria commodities such as ACTs and RDTs based upon real-time data. Better tools including detailed topographical maps are needed to improve targeting of malaria resources.

Plans and Justification

President's Malaria Initiative will continue to provide technical assistance in improving the overall surveillance systems, which includes the HMIS and the PHEM. However, as these systems are not yet fully functional, PMI will continue to enhance these capabilities and support the ten epidemic detection sites in Oromia and if necessary, provide technical assistance for establishing additional enhanced malaria surveillance sites where resistance to antimalarial medications and insecticides will also be monitored. Furthermore, PMI will continue to conduct annual national malaria commodities microplans. PMI will continue to support nationally representative surveys to obtain key PMI coverage outcome indicators periodically and explore other diagnostic tools e.g., serology to monitor progress in Ethiopia.

Proposed Activities with FY 2014 Funding ($1,524,200):

• **Epidemic Detection and Surveillance Sites: ($300,000):** PMI will continue to support the network of ten epidemic detection sites established in 2010 including enhanced surveillance and malaria epidemic detection capacities and weekly electronic reporting from health posts.

• **Strengthening Routine Epidemic Detection and Surveillance ($200,000):** PMI will continue to strengthen the capacity of community-level HEWs and HEW supervisors to detect and respond to increases in malaria caseloads or epidemic outbreaks at the community level and HEW supervisor training, integrated supervisions and regular field visits in 293 districts in six regional states (approximately one third of the country). The purpose of the activity is to strengthen surveillance in the health care delivery system as a whole, leveraging the project's reach and ability to communicate with regards to occurring epidemic outbreaks, thereby ensuring a timely response. When outbreaks are detected at community level, PMI will ensure that ORHB, FMOH, and EHNRI are notified, so that a coordinated response can be implemented. If new approaches to improve epidemic surveillance are found to be effective (e.g., mapping of malaria micro clusters; school based surveillance), this project platform will be used to scale-up these approaches to national level.

• **National Malaria Commodities Microplan: ($350,000)** PMI will continue to support an annual malaria commodities' microplan for all of Ethiopia's regional states. At least 700 district staff cognizant of malaria burden will attend regional meetings once annually to present and compile these data. It is the main malaria commodity planning, distribution and tracking tool for all PMI and non-PMI supported commodity procurements as well as providing malaria data.

• **Strengthening data management capacity ($100,000):** The FMOH has various systems for obtaining health data ranging from HMIS, PHEM system reports, and other fiscal, laboratory and supply chain reports. There are gaps in capacity to analyze data and reports, and to complete requests for additional funding from various malaria donors. PMI will support the FMOH to address these data management capacity gaps.

• **Strengthening reporting from health post level ($400,000):** Through PEPFAR funding, GoE has established enhanced health management information systems in 143 malaria hotspot districts at the health center level in the country. With FY 2014 funding, PMI will strengthen reporting of malaria cases from the health post to the health centers in these districts to strengthen malaria epidemic detection and response which is not captured in the current system. The lessons learned from the ESR SMS system will inform this activity.

• **M&E and OR CDC TDYs ($24,200):** Two TDY visits to provide technical assistance for surveillance, M&E activities and/or operational research studies.

• **FELTP: ($150,000)** The GoE has requested that the FELTP expand to accommodate 23 trainees annually. Substantial malaria projects involving FELTP residents began in 2011 in Ethiopia. PMI will continue to support at least three trainees who will focus their field training on malaria prevention and control, including malaria outbreak detection and response activities, and an evaluation of malaria surveillance efforts.

SOCIAL AND BEHAVIOR CHANGE COMMUNICATION (SBCC)

NMCP/PMI Objectives

Key objectives for SBCC are to increase community knowledge regarding malaria prevention, diagnosis, treatment, and control, especially relating to: (i) the establishment of a culture of correct and consistent LLIN use; (ii) increased community awareness about the effectiveness of IRS and the need to reduce re-plastering of walls; and (iii) improved treatment-seeking behavior for fever. The HEP offers a highly effective opportunity to provide nationwide information and conduct SBCC activities to improve LLIN use in nearly all malaria endemic communities across

Ethiopia. To consolidate the gains and further enhance the effectiveness of HEP, the government has designed a scaling up strategy which will be implemented through organizing a Health Development Army (HDA). The HDAs will support HEWs to increase contact with each household through networking one to five households in a more detailed way. This would provide a significantly important opportunity to increase LLIN use in each *kebele*. PMI-funded SBCC activities began in FY 2009. These activities are supporting HEWs with communications materials and training. The SBCC activities provide malaria-specific materials and trainings through a wide range of community based organizations, schools, HDAs, women's groups, churches, NGOs and other networks of civil society.

Progress during the Last 12 Months

Since 2009, PMI has provided assistance to the GoE to carry out malaria behavior change communication activities. Working with the HEP, zonal, and district offices and HDAs, PMI has delivered critical link to SBCC activities. PMI has provided funds to support the HEP to work with families at the village and community level under the Model Families Program to educate Ethiopian families to take specific actions to protect themselves against malaria. This program includes HDAs who work under direction of HEWs to support their communities, families, and schools to take necessary actions to prevent malaria.

During the first half of 2013, a total of 1,781, 614 SBCC materials have been distributed. The distributed materials include; malaria scorecards, malaria flipcharts, malaria protection stickers, 'how to hang a LLIN' leaflets, malaria posters, ANC training manuals, ANC booklets, Amharic scorecards, heroine cards, husband invitation cards, and ANC posters. As a result of this effort, a total of 96,755 households were reached. Again, 11,760 HDAs and community leaders received briefing sessions to enable them to implement SBCC activities. In addition, a total of 2,512 students have been reached through school clubs and another 26,180 students through school mini-media in a total of 60 schools. As part of capacity building in malaria key messaging, 771 health service provider and 1,256 HEWs were trained.

The LLIN hang-up assist campaigns have been executed within seventeen districts involving a total of 399,100 LLINs since 2010. Since 2010, eight hang-up campaigns have been carried out, in partnership with CJTF-HOA, successfully hanging a total of over 200,000 nets in eight districts of Oromia Regional State. Between June 2012 and June 2013, these projects were conducted in ten districts assisting hang-up of over 173,000 LLINs.

Challenges, Opportunities and Threats

The recent Ethiopia 2011 DHS shows the level of exposure to mass media is low in Ethiopia. Only 22 % of women and 38% of men listen to the radio at least once a week. In addition, 68% of women aged 15–49 and 54% of men in the same age group didn't have access to any of the three common media types (TV, radio, or print).

Malaria SBCC message harmonization and standardization also remains a challenge, as there is no dedicated office within the FMOH that coordinates and provides professional leadership for these activities. There is strong need to work at national level to produce messages according to the national standards. This can be achieved through SBCC technical working group and bringing SBCC partners under the same platform. Low bed net utilization and slow replacement of nets is still a challenge in demand creation efforts. Cultural factors that may determine ownership and use of LLINs must be taken into consideration to ensure that communication and advocacy activities contribute to effective use of LLINs. Misuse of LLINs and not sleeping under LLINs has frequently been reported anecdotally.

Plans and Justification

With FY 2014 funding, malaria SBCC activities will be more integrated and coordinated with other health behavioral change communication (BCC) activities for PMTCT, TB, FP/RH, MNCH, and nutrition. PMI will also support local organizations through Annual Program Statement (APS) mechanism to build local capacity in malaria key message communications.

Social behavior change communication partners will review the choice of media channels based on evidence. Interpersonal communication such as entertainment education, using school, and religious institutions will be encouraged. Promotional efforts on consistent and proper ITN use will use alternative SBCC interventions that can reach target groups with no access to radio and television. Suggested interventions include video, school programs, and community meetings, as well as other creative methods. Focus will be put on strategies initiated by the communities themselves, i.e., through HDAs and the Focal Parents program that is overseen by HEWs.

Social behavior change communication activities through mass media and rural communications campaigns, supporting community level change agents like HDAs, can be applied in an integrated fashion for the other interventions (e.g., ACTs, IRS). For communications activities related to RDTs and ACTs in particular, PMI will work with health providers at different levels of the health system to strengthen their interpersonal communication skills. The SBCC strategy may follow any behavioral framework that is appropriate for the Ethiopia situation. An example of a framework that may offer a way to organize the SBCC approach is the so called "Essential Malaria Actions" which will also supplement the SBCC activities of HDAs and HEWs.

Proposed Activities with FY 2014 Funding ($1,400,000)

PMI will seek to make use of interpersonal communication channels to deliver malaria messages and work through a wide range of implementing partners and in-country stakeholders including HEWs and HDAs at the community level. Additionally, PMI will continue to provide SBCC materials developed to other implementing organizations, so that reach of these materials can be maximized.

• **Social Behavior Change Communication ($1,000,000):** With FY 2014 funding, PMI will continue to support the implementation of malaria-specific SBCC messages through a range of different channels, including community conversations, house-to-house visits, school health programs, and limited mass media targeting specific groups, which will be tailored based on the assessment results. With FY 2014 funding, PMI will continue to support the dissemination of those messages beyond Oromia into all regional states of the country and trainings on SBCC and developed materials will be given to FMOH staff from all regional states and zones as well as from partner organizations. Partners will be trained in the various SBCC approaches, how to disseminate the messages, and how to measure their impact in terms of malaria knowledge and behavior change.

• **Community-based SBCC ($400,000):** With FY 2014 funding, PMI will support local organizations to carry out community based BCC activities in selected *woredas* of Oromia Regional State. This activity will target school communities, faith-based organizations (FBOs) and local media. This will help to reinforce and complement the HDAs community based interpersonal behavioral change interventions.

CAPACITY BUILDING & HEALTH SYSTEMS STRENGTHENING

NMCP/PMI Objectives

Ethiopia faces many challenges related to human resources for healthcare, including the shortage of skilled health workers, high turnover, and lack retention of health professionals in remote and inaccessible health facilities where malaria is prevalent. Decentralization of the health care system places an additional management burden on the Zonal and District Health Offices. While it is beyond the ability of PMI to address the system-wide capacity issues, there are areas within the NMCP where capacity can be strengthened, including through pre- and in-service refresher trainings. The Ethiopian Human Resource for Health (HRH) strategy aimed to develop and maintain a health workforce that is appropriately sized, skilled, well-balanced, distributed, resourced, and performing efficiently and effectively in order to provide all Ethiopians with equal access to a minimum health care package, sufficient to meet Ethiopians health development targets in a fiscally responsible manner.

Progress during the Last 12 Months

The FMOH HRH Strategy was released in June 2010. PMI supports this strategy through support for pre- and in-service training curriculum for HEWs and other healthcare workers, to include best practices in malaria diagnosis and treatment. PMI collaborated with partners to strengthen the capacity of the ORHB and FMOH staff and others at the national, district and community levels to plan, implement, supervise, monitor and evaluate malaria prevention and control activities. The April 2013 program review indicated that as of March 2013, 647 health care workers (46% of the annual target) were trained in malaria through in-service training. In addition, a rapid situational assessment and baseline assessment were finalized. Standard guidelines were developed for midwifery, anesthesia and HEWs human resource development programs. Moreover, 42 schools received a capacity building training on infrastructure, teaching and learning materials. As a response to FMOH priorities, problem-based learning workshop has been conducted for universities and medical colleges that are implementing the new medical curriculum. Assessment of the human resource management capacity of the ministry and curriculum development for health education institutions have been carried out during this fiscal year.

Challenges, Opportunities and Threats

The high turnover rate at FMOH and limited human resources capacities of RHBs are commonly mentioned as challenges for this effort. In addition, ORHB identified coordination of implementing partners as a major challenge. This has limited the progress of malaria control in Oromia through overlapping coverage in some areas with poor coverage in others, inadequate data sharing for partners to monitor progress and poor utility of existing resources.

Plans and Justification

There is a need to support ORHB to improve coordination with malaria stakeholders through coordination meetings, joint planning, supportive supervision for district level program implementation, and public symposia to share program updates, challenges and best practices.

Proposed Activities with FY 2014 Funding ($100,000)

• **Coordination support for ORHB ($100,000):** Support joint planning, coordination, support supervision and review activities with all malaria stakeholders in Oromia Regional Health Bureau.

STAFFING AND ADMINISTRATION

Two health professionals serve as Resident Advisors (RAs) to oversee PMI in Ethiopia, one representing CDC and one representing USAID. Five Foreign Service Nationals were hired to support the PMI team: one Senior Malaria Advisor, one Malaria Advisor, a Malaria & HIV specialist, an SBCC Specialist, and one Program Manager. All PMI staff members are part of a single interagency team led by the USAID Mission Director or his/her designee in country. The PMI team shares responsibility for development and implementation of PMI strategies and work plans, coordination with national authorities, managing collaborating agencies and supervising day-to-day activities. Candidates for resident advisor positions (whether initial hires or replacements) will be evaluated and/or interviewed jointly by USAID and CDC, and both agencies will be involved in hiring decisions, with the final decision made by the individual agency.

PMI professional staff work together to oversee all technical and administrative aspects of PMI, including finalizing details of the project design, implementing malaria prevention and treatment activities, monitoring and evaluation of outcomes and impact, reporting of results, and providing guidance to PMI partners.

The PMI lead in country is the USAID/Ethiopia Mission Director. The two PMI RAs, one from USAID and one from CDC, report to the Senior USAID Health Officer for day-to-day leadership, and work together as a part of a single interagency team. The technical expertise housed in Atlanta and Washington guides PMI programmatic efforts and thus overall technical guidance for both RAs falls to PMI staff in Atlanta and Washington. Since CDC resident advisors are CDC employees (CDC USDD—38), responsibility for completing official performance reviews lies with the CDC Country Director who is expected to rely upon input from PMI staff across the two agencies that work closely day in and day out with the CDC RA and thus best positioned to comment on the RA's performance.

The two PMI resident advisors are based within the USAID health office and are expected to spend approximately half their time sitting with and providing technical assistance to the national and regional malaria control programs and partners.

Locally-hired staff to support PMI activities either in Ministries or in USAID will be approved by the USAID Mission Director. Because of the need to adhere to specific country policies and USAID accounting regulations, any transfer of PMI funds directly to Ministries or host governments will need to be approved by the USAID Mission Director and Controller, in addition to the PMI Coordinator.

Description and Budget for Proposed Activities with FY 2014 funding ($2,150,000)

1. **Management of PMI ($2,150,000):** Support to seven staff members, including two senior Resident Advisors (one USAID and one CDC) based at the USAID Mission within the U.S. embassy in Addis Ababa. The support includes all work-related expenses (e.g., salaries, travel, supplies, etc.), and mission-based expenditures, including USAID mission expenses incurred in the direct implementation of PMI activities.

Table I

President's Malaria Initiative – *Ethiopia*
Year 7 (FY2014) Budget Breakdowns by Partner ($37,000,000)

Partner Organization	Geographic Area	Activity	Budget
Abt Associates Public-Private Partnerships (PPP)	Amhara & Oromia	Private sector support to case management training	$100,000
APS	Oromia/National	APS for local implementation of BCC campaigns	$400,000
CDC *IAA*	National	In-country staff; administrative expenses, TDYs, entomology supplies and equipment	$608,400
G2G	National	PFSA strengthening, Strengthening data management capacity, Coordination support for ORHB	$450,000
JHPIEGO HRH	National	Expanding malaria in pregnancy services through safe motherhood and FANC	$300,000
ICAP	Oromia/National	Support for QA system for malaria laboratory diagnosis	$900,000
TBD	Oromia	Procurement of IRS equipment; IRS operations; Entomological monitoring and capacity-building	$3,600,000
L10K	Three zones	iCCM in three zones	$550,000
TBD	National	Epidemic surveillance and response	$200,000
PMI/Ethiopia RFQ	Oromia	Procurement of IRS insecticides	$4,500,000
SIAPS	National	Strengthening of drug management system capacity	$750,000
TBD	National	LLIN distribution to health posts	$300,000

TBD	National	Provide systems support for ongoing supervision and monitoring of malaria treatment	$600,000
TBD	Oromia	Maintenance of epidemic detection sites	$300,000
TBD	National	Strengthening reporting of data from health posts	$400,000
TBD	Oromia/National	SBCC for LLINs, IRS, ACTs, case management	$1,000,000
UNICEF	Oromia/National	Procurement and distribution of LLINs, RDTs, lab equipment and supplies, ACTs, chloroquine, pre-referral and severe antimalarial drugs, primaquine; support for national commodities' microplanning	$19,891,600
USP *PQM*	National	Strengthen drug quality monitoring	$400,000
Total			$37,000,000

Table II

President's Malaria Initiative – *Ethiopia*

Planned Obligations for FY 2014 ($37,000,000)

Proposed Activity	Mechanism	Budget	Commodities	Geographic area	Description of Activity
PREVENTION					
INSECTICIDE-TREATED BED NETS					
LLIN procurement and distribution	UNICEF	8,491,600	8,491,600	Oromia/National	Provide 2,100,000 free LLINs through health facilities, HEWs and other networks at approx. $3.50/net procurement plus $0.50/net for distribution to district
LLIN distribution from districts to health posts	TBD	300,000		National	LLIN distribution from districts to health posts at $0.15/net
Subtotal		8,791,600	8,491,600		
INDOOR RESIDUAL SPRAYING					
Insecticide procurement	PMI/Ethiopia RFQ	4,500,000	4,500,000	Oromia	Procurement of insecticide for IRS activities
IRS operations	TBD	3,000,000	250,000	Oromia	Training, implementation and supervision support for IRS operations targeting 550,000 structures; procurement of spray equipment and personal protective gear
IRS training	TBD	100,000		National	Building the national capacity for IRS operations planning and management, environmental compliance and poison control
Entomological monitoring and capacity-building	TBD	500,000		National	Sustaining capacity for entomological monitoring for vector control

Proposed Activity	Mechanism	Budget	Commodities	Geographic area	Description of Activity
ENTOMOLOGICAL MONITORING					
Entomological supplies and equipment	CDC IAA	10,000	10,000	National	Provide critical supplies, reagents and equipment for routine entomological monitoring activities and resistance and bionomic studies.
Entomological technical assistance	CDC IAA	24,200		National	Provide two TA visits from CDC/Atlanta for training, planning and monitoring entomological activities.
Subtotal		8,134,200	4,760,000		
MALARIA IN PREGNANCY					
Expanding malaria in pregnancy services through safe motherhood and FANC	JHPIEGO HRH	300,000		National	Pre-service training of HEWs & midwives to ensure that malaria will be focused in pre- and in-service training for management of acute malaria in pregnant women.
Subtotal		300,000			
Subtotal Prevention		17,225,800	13,251,600		
CASE MANAGEMENT					
DIAGNOSIS					
Procurement of RDTs	UNICEF	4,800,000	4,800,000	Oromia/National	Procurement and distribution of 6,000,000 RDTs to support FMOH/ORHB efforts to scale-up RDT use at the health facility level
Support for QA system for malaria laboratory diagnosis	ICAP	900,000		Oromia/National	This will include support for refresher training, supervision, other QA/QC activities, and program monitoring. Training and accreditation will be provided to laboratory supervisors.
Procurement of laboratory equipment/supplies	UNICEF	750,000	750,000	Oromia	Procurement of laboratory equipment and supplies (e.g., microscopes), and including logistics systems support

	Partner	Amount	Amount	Location	Description
Subtotal		6,450,000	5,550,000		
TREATMENT					
Procurement of ACTs, chloroquine, pre-referral treatment and drugs for severe malaria, and primaquine	UNICEF	5,500,000	5,500,000	Oromia/National	Procurement of ACTs, chloroquine, primaquine, pre-referral treatment and drugs for severe malaria
Provide systems support for ongoing supervision and monitoring of malaria treatment	TBD	600,000		National	Support for health worker supervision for management of malaria at district-level health centers and community-level health posts; collaboration with Zonal and District Health Offices
Private sector support to case management training	Abt Associates PPP	100,000		Amhara & Oromia	Work with the RHBs and private health facilities in Amhara and Oromia to increase access to quality malaria services
iCCM in three zones	L10K	550,000		Three zones	Integrated community case management support in three zones
Subtotal		6,750,000	5,500,000		
PHARMACEUTICAL MANAGEMENT					
Strengthening of drug management system	SIAPS	750,000		National	Strengthening of drug management system, quantification and procurement; distribution management; and health facility drug availability
PFSA strengthening	G2G	250,000		National	Strengthening PFSA pharmaceutical management capacities
Strengthen drug quality monitoring	USP *PQM*	400,000	70,000	National	Support to FMHACA for monitoring of post marketing anti-malarial drug quality regionally and nationally
Subtotal		1,400,000	70,000		
Subtotal Case Management		14,600,000	11,120,000		
MONITORING AND EVALUATION					

Activity	Funding	Budget		Location	Description
Maintenance of Epidemic Detection & Surveillance Sites	TBD	300,000		Oromia	Maintain epidemic detection sites, reporting both district and community-level data on malaria morbidity and mortality, as well as data on occurrence of transmission micro-clusters, patient access, and commodity use
Epidemic surveillance and response	TBD	200,000		National	Support for ESR planning at district and zonal level; support for surveillance system; operational costs; reserve stocks for LLINs, RDTs and drugs budgeted in prevention and case management sections
National malaria commodities microplan	UNICEF	350,000		National	Expansion of yearly malaria commodity microplan as done in Oromia
Strengthening data management capacity	G2G	100,000		National	Support to address data management capacity gaps
Strengthening reporting of data from health posts	TBD	400,000		National	Strengthen reporting of malaria cases from the health post to the health centers in hotspot districts to strengthen malaria epidemic detection and response
M&E and OR technical assistance	CDC IAA	24,200		National	Two TDY trips to support M&E and OR activities
Field Epidemiology & Laboratory Training Program (FELTP)	CDC IAA	150,000		National	Support for applied epidemiology and laboratory training for FMOH staff
Subtotal Monitoring and Evaluation		1,524,200			
SBCC					
SBCC for LLINs, IRS, ACTs, case management	TBD	1,000,000	25,000	National	Training, dissemination and implementation of various SBCC approaches through a variety of platforms
Community-based SBCC	APS	400,000		Oromia/National	Community-based behavioral communication through schools and FBOs for prevention and control of malaria
Subtotal SBCC		1,400,000	25,000		
CAPACITY BUILDING					
Coordination support for ORHB	G2G	100,000		Oromia	Support joint planning, coordination, support supervision

				and review activities with all malaria stakeholders in ORHB
Subtotal Capacity Building			100,000	
STAFFING AND ADMINISTRATION				
In-country staff; Admin. Expenses	CDC *IAA*	400,000		Salaries, benefits of in-country CDC PMI staff (1)
In-country staff; Admin. Expenses	USAID	1,750,000		Salaries, benefits of in-country USAID PMI staff (1 PSC / 5 FSNs); ICASS support of CDC PMI staff
Subtotal Staffing and Administration		2,150,000		
TOTAL		37,000,000	24,396,600	**Commodities (66%)**